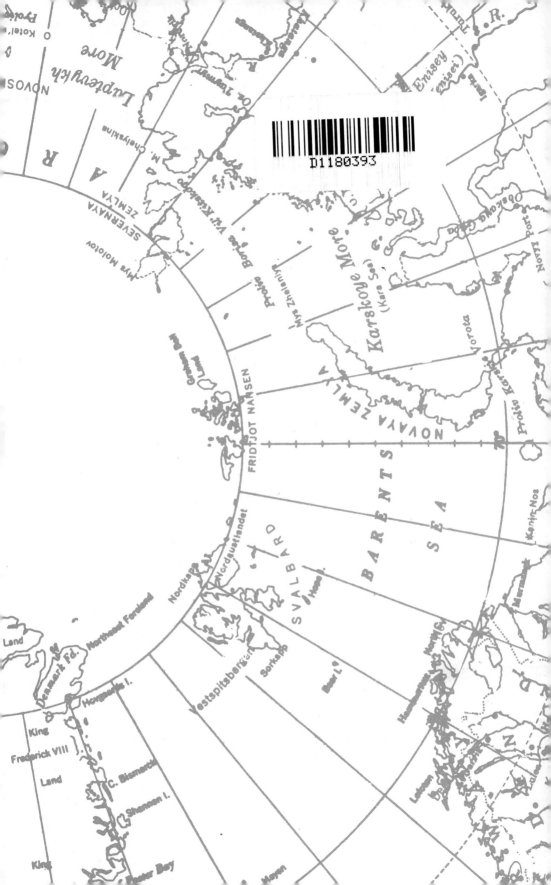

UNITED STATES
POLAR
EXPLORATION

National Archives Conference

Volume I

(Papers of the) Conference
on
United States Polar Exploration

Washington D.C., 1967.

NATIONAL ARCHIVES AND RECORDS SERVICE

September 8, 1967
The National Archives Building
Washington, D.C.

NATIONAL ARCHIVES

CONFERENCES

UNITED STATES POLAR EXPLORATION

EDITED BY

Herman R. Friis

AND

Shelby G. Bale, Jr.

Ohio University Press

ATHENS, OHIO

PUBLISHED BY OHIO UNIVERSITY PRESS FOR
THE NATIONAL ARCHIVES TRUST FUND BOARD
NATIONAL ARCHIVES AND RECORDS SERVICE
GENERAL SERVICES ADMINISTRATION
WASHINGTON: 1970

LIBRARY OF CONGRESS CARD CATALOG NO. 70-141379
ISBN 8214-0093-2

CONTENTS

SESSION II
Highlights of United States Exploration
and Research in Antarctica

SESSION III
Writing and Research on Antarctica

SESSION IV
Writing and Research on the Arctic

SESSION V
Visual Records of Polar Explorations

Concluding Session

LIST OF ILLUSTRATIONS

FOREWORD

In 1967, the National Archives and Records Service inaugurated a series of conferences for the exchange of ideas and information between archivists and researchers. These conferences are designed to inform scholars about the wealth of useful research materials available in the National Archives and Records Service, as well as to provide an opportunity for researchers to suggest ways in which their use of these records could be facilitated.

The National Archives and Records Service, a part of the General Services Administration, administers the permanently valuable, noncurrent records of the Federal Government. These archival holdings date from the days of the Continental Congresses to the present.

Among the 900,000 cubic feet of records now constituting the National Archives of the United States are hallowed documents such as the Declaration of Independence, the Constitution, and the Bill of Rights. However, most of the archives, whether in the National Archives Building, the Federal Records Centers, or the Presidential Libraries, are less dramatic. They are preserved because of their continuing practical utility for the ordinary processes of government, for the establishment and protection of individual rights, and for casting light on our Nation's history when subjected to the scrutiny of the diligent scholar.

One goal of the National Archives staff is to explore and make more widely known these historical records. It is hoped that these conferences will be a positive act in that direction. The proceedings of each conference will be published, in the belief that this lively exchange of ideas and information should be preserved and made available in printed form.

ROBERT L. KUNZIG
Administrator of General Services

PREFACE

The Conference on United States Polar Exploration, held on September 8, 1967, and attended by more than two hundred persons, formally opened the Center for Polar Archives in the National Archives. The conference consisted of five sessions during the day, each session made up of a chairman, speakers, and commentators. The program format did not provide for questions from the floor or general discussions. The concluding session, which was held in the evening, consisted of the conference's main address and the opening of the United States Polar Exploration exhibit.

Increased activity in the Arctic and Antarctic by the United States Government and its citizens since World War II (particularly since the International Geophysical Year, 1957-58) has resulted in the creation of more Federal records and private papers pertaining to polar matters than ever before. Their importance as a segment of our national heritage continues to grow with the passage of time and in the context of our rapidly expanding body of scientific knowledge. The Center is designed to serve as a depository both for private collections of polar papers and for records created by the Federal agencies involved in polar exploration and research. Here they will be preserved in a properly controlled archival environment and will be made available to scholars for research, subject in some cases to restrictions placed on them by the private donor or the Federal agency that created them.

The purpose of this conference, in addition to opening the Center for Polar Archives, was to call to the attention of those involved in polar activities the availability of this specialized archival facility and to notify scholars that some Federal records and private papers are already here. Our preservation of the records is of little value unless they are used for research.

The Center for Polar Archives and the Conference on United States Polar Exploration were the result of enterprising work by many persons. Both, however, originated from Herman Friis' long-held interest in the polar regions and his adherence to the principle that records of man's activities should be preserved for use by scholars of this and future generations.

JAMES B. RHOADS
Archivist of the United States

INTRODUCTION

The Conference on United States Polar Exploration not only marked the beginning of the Conference Series of the National Archives; it also marked the founding of the Center for Polar Archives. The purposes of both the conference and the Center were to recognize the significant role of the United States in polar exploration and to ensure the preservation of the priceless cultural and scientific heritage that records the accomplishments of men and women throughout the history of United States polar exploration.

On this occasion the National Archives was honored by the attendance of what was one of the largest gatherings of leaders in this field. Many of these men and women played a vital role as participants in the effort to explore and document the vast polar regions. Through their support they have added immeasurably to the success of the Center for Polar Archives.

The response to the conference and to the creation of the Center for Polar Archieves has been both favorable and encouraging. Since the conference the Center has received numerous donations of private papers, amounting to approximately 500,000 items and consisting of correspondence, diaries, notebooks, aerial photographs, still and motion pictures, maps, paintings, and museum-type objects. With one of these gifts is perhaps the first sound recording of the noises of seals, skuas, and penguins in the Bay of Whales, Antarctica, in 1934-35; another collection includes the recording of the voice of a famous explorer shortly after his return from an early twentieth-century expedition into the highest latitudes of the Arctic. Among the museum-type items included in the Center's collections are a few navigational instruments, flags, a camp stove, and several pieces of scrimshaw.

The larger accessions represent the collections of Admiral Robert E. Peary, Dr. Paul A. Siple, Dr. James E. Mooney, Captain Harold E. Saunders, and Dr. Russell W. Porter. The size of a collection, however, does not necessarily determine its significance: a single manuscript sheet with a record of meteorological and position-reckoning information recorded during a historic trans-Antarctic flight can be a valuable contribution to understanding the role of science in early twentieth-century explorations.

As a result of these gifts a number of U.S. expeditions to the polar regions are well documented by papers in the Center. There is, for example, abundant information concerning the Arctic expeditions of Admiral Peary and men who were associated with him, such as Mr. George H. Clark, General Thomas Hubbard, Mr. Hugh J. Lee, Dr. Russell W. Porter, and Mr. J. S. Warmbath. The Antarctic is also well represented in the Center. The papers of Dr. Dana Coman, Mr. Stevenson Corey, Dr. Alton Lindsey, Captain Finn Ronne, Captain Harold E. Saunders, and Dr. Paul A. Siple provide detailed and voluminous data for the study of Richard E. Byrd's expeditions of 1928-30 and 1933-35.

In addition to personal papers the Center has accessioned official records. These include records of the *Polaris* Expedition of 1871-73, the *Jeannette* Expedition of 1879-82, the Lady Franklin Bay Expedition of 1881-84, and the U.S. Antarctic Service Expedition of 1939-41.

Each collection retains its physical unity as accessioned. Within each collection the holdings are preliminarily arranged according to category of material; for example, correspondence, journals and notebooks, and observational data. Thus it is possible to readily cross-reference requests for information about the total holdings of the Center.

The success of this conference and the development of the Center owes much to the continuous support and encouragement of Dr. Robert H. Bahmer, Archivist of the United States from 1966-68, and of his Deputy, Dr. James Berton Rhoads, who has been Archivist of the United States since 1968. Dr. E. G. Campbell, Assistant Archivist of the United States, has been instrumental in guiding both the Center and the conference.

Mr. Shelby G. Bale, Jr., is to be commended for his role as manuscript editor of the papers presented at the conference and for transcribing the tapes of conference proceedings. For the logistical success of the conference, Mr. Albert Leisinger and members of his staff in the former Division of Exhibits and Publications must be thanked. Most recently, Dr. Frank Burke and the editorial staff of the Educational Programs Division have been responsible for the publication of conference papers through the Ohio University Press.

Mr. George Curtis, who joined the staff of the Center in 1971, has been successful in the development of a responsive accessioning program and in initiating a comprehensive plan for the arrangement of collections of papers.

The most valuable and capable assistance in bringing both the Conference on United States Polar Exploration and this publication of its papers to a successful conclusion was provided by Miss Alison Wilson, who has been with the Center for Polar Archives since its beginning and has worked tirelessly for the success of all its programs.

HERMAN R. FRIIS
Conference Director

UNITED STATES
POLAR
EXPLORATION

WELCOME

Robert H. Bahmer

Archivist of the United States, 1966–68

It is a pleasure for me to welcome all of you to the National Archives and to the Conference on United States Polar Exploration. We are honored indeed to have such a distinguished group of guests at the first of a series of conferences at the National Archives in various subject matter fields in which we feel that we can make some contributions. I want to take this opportunity to personally thank all of the conference participants for giving so generously of their time and talent in making this program possible.

One of the primary missions of the National Archives is, of course, the preservation of the records of our past. We are in a sense the collective memory of our Nation. All of us in the National Archives are happy that it has been possible for us to provide an appropriate place in our institution for the public and private records of U.S. polar exploration. Our interest in records, however, goes beyond their mere physical preservation. We are interested in facilitating the use of the records in our custody. Without research and study, the existence of these records means little or nothing. We play no favorites in facilitating research in our records, which are as varied as the activities of the Government they document. However, it probably will be no surprise to any of you to hear that those records documenting the political and diplomatic activities of our Nation are used more than any other records. I hope that this conference will highlight our interest in facilitating research in the records of our Nation's scientific efforts. While I am no expert on the subject, I do know that the records of polar exploration contain information in a number of disciplines—geology, geography, botany, zoology, ecology, etc. To the layman, these records have, I suppose, an additional interest—one that we could perhaps call inspirational.

We have all been thrilled as children and as adults by the stories of our Nation's beginning—the tales of our heroic battles for freedom and the exploits of the pioneers who, in their westward march, settled the continent. However, I know of no activity in which we have participated that offers more evidence of indomitable courage, steadfast faith, and unconquerable will than the feats of arctic and antarctic exploration; and we have not come to the end of that chapter of our history. While we probably shall never again see individual achievements like Peary's sledge drive to the North Pole or Byrd's lonely winter at Little America in Antarctica, there are today, as you know, brave men and women working in the Arctic and Antarctic. Their contributions to scientific knowledge will undoubtedly be impressive.

Let me again say thank you for coming. At this point I should like to turn the program over to my colleague, the man who is chiefly responsible for your being here today. His interest in exploration and research in the polar regions dates back a good many years, and his friendships and associations with many of you are numerous. It was his idea that we establish the Center for Polar Archives. I am happy that this, one of his many visions, has finally come to fruition after a considerable number of years of effort on his part.

Herman Friis is one of those remarkable persons who is a true scholar in the best tradition of American scholarship, and he has the enviable position of having earned the respect of his colleagues both in the archival profession and in the subject matter disciplines of cartography and geography. I am pleased to turn the program over to my colleague, Herman Friis.

THE CENTER FOR POLAR ARCHIVES

Herman R. Friis

During World War II, Mr. Friis prepared regional terrain studies, histories of scientific exploration, and cartographic studies of the Arctic and served as officer in charge of the Cartographic Branch of the Arctic, Desert, and Tropic Information Center. Since joining the staff of the National Archives in 1938 he has been Chief of the Cartographic Division and Chief of the Technical Records Division. Currently he is Director of the Center for Polar Archives.

In 1789 John Churchman, Government clerk, surveyor-mathematician, and imaginative geophysicist of sorts, petitioned the First U.S. Congress to subsidize his proposed expedition to Baffin Bay. He continued to petition the First Congress when no funds were granted to him. In 1791 he asked for $3,000 to acquire two 130-ton ships and to maintain an expedition to Baffin Bay so that he could carry out observations for longitude and latitude, verify his theories concerning magnetic variation, and ". . . extend the researches for more satisfactorily deciding on the existence of a north-westerly passage into the Pacific Ocean."[1] The First Congress, faced with many problems and innumerable domestic tasks, again responded with an emphatic negative. Thus died in successive select committees this Nation's first attempts for an official scientific expedition to the polar regions.

From this feeble, ill-fated beginning there has evolved a history of a maturing national appreciation and eventual recognition of the importance of the polar regions. The first interest was a response to the economies of whaling, sealing, and the China trade; then a response to national pride and a search for prestige in reaching the

---

[1] *A Record of the Reports of Select Committees of the House of Representatives of the United States,* Vol. 1, p. 75, Record Group 233, Records of the U.S. House of Representatives, National Archives.

poles and in exploring and claiming new lands; and most recently, a response to the need of our complex present-day world society for maximum knowledge of total environment. The resultant body of records forming the history of U.S. polar accomplishments is large —far larger than most of us may realize. A purpose of the conference today is to have the highlights of this history illuminated by some of our colleagues who are authorities on the subject as a result of their field experience and scientific research. It is also our purpose to emphasize the importance of preserving and describing the records of this history.

Those of us who have examined and have used the records of these many accomplishments are impressed by the explorer's sensitive appreciation of the need to preserve his own and his associates' accounts—be they journals, logbooks, diaries, correspondence, reports, observations, photographs, maps, or other types of records. Fortunately for posterity, this appreciation and the desire in most of us to be identified with our achievements have been responsible for the large treasure trove of official records and private papers that have been preserved in a wide variety of depositories throughout the country.

You will perhaps recall Elisha Kent Kane's poignant remarks in his report to the Secretary of the Navy upon his return from commanding the Second Grinnell Expedition, 1853-55. He and his small party had abandoned their ship, the *Advance,* in May, 1855. During their 5-month escape south, dragging their sledges and subsisting on limited rations, they were forced by the cold and by numbing fatigue to abandon most of their gear and practically all of their treasured collections. Their own survival was at stake. In Kane's official report he recorded that:

> We were able, not without difficulty, to carry our chronometers and the various instruments, magnetic and others, which might allow me still to make and verify our accustomed observations. We left behind the theodolite of the United States Coast Survey and the valuable self-registering barometric apparatus furnished by the American Philosophical Society. Our library, as well as those portions which had been furnished by the government and by Mr. Grinnell as my own, were necessarily sacrificed. We preserved only the documents of the Expedition.[2]

[2] Elisha Kent Kane, *Arctic Explorations in the Years 1853, '54, '55*, Vol. 2 (Philadelphia, 1856), p. 314.

Many of these documents of the expedition, so painfully retained and protected, were turned over to the Navy Department. This practice has been followed with few exceptions. For example, the documents of the *Jeannette* exploring expedition under Lieutenant George Washington DeLong, of the U.S. Expedition to Lady Franklin Bay under Lieutenant Adolphus W. Greely, and of innumerable expeditions before and since, under similar circumstances, despite all odds, have been preserved. Various circumstances, however, have worked against the centralization of the total official record. A sizable portion of the total record is found in the personal papers of individuals who took part in these activities. As personal papers they have remained in personal custody and, accordingly, have become widely dispersed; some, indeed, over the years have been lost.

For example, a survey of extant papers of the Second Grinnell Expedition indicates that there are manuscripts in the National Archives, the Chester County Historical Society, the National Geographic Society, the Library of Congress, a private collection in Washington, D.C., and, interestingly, in Glassboro State College. A survey of the extant records of the United States Exploring Expedition commanded by Lieutenant Charles Wilkes, 1838-42, reveals that they may be found in at least twenty-five different depositories.

We do not know how many of the papers of these and other expeditions are in attics, in trunks, or perhaps framed in someone's living room or den. But their number must be legion. As unique items these documents are tangible proof of a happening, a record however small or however large of an event in the history of civilization. Their identification and preservation should be a matter of primary concern to all of us. Where are they?

The chief aim of polar exploration is the increase of knowledge; without this there would be few benefits, and the effort would soon become a memory. Contribution to knowledge takes many forms, one of which is publication. Most of us want to publish an account of our research and travels. Where, for example, are the published papers of James Eights, perhaps the first U.S. scientist to visit and to do fieldwork in Antarctica? In what periodicals and other scientific publications were they published? Where are the publications that were produced by members of all U.S. expeditions and stations before 1942? The literature in this field is as considerable as the subjects are wide ranging. Yet, here may well be the most useful overall record. It is the basis for our knowledge of the history of the discovery and development of the polar regions.

Mindful of the rich resource of official U.S. records and of the personal papers of scientists and others who have served in the broad field of polar activities, and mindful of the critical need to preserve these records, the Archivist of the United States has established the Center for Polar Archives. Among its objectives and functions are: the collection, preservation, and description of official records and personal papers; the compilation and publication of a list of all U.S. official and private expeditions and programs in the polar regions; the compilation of an inventory locating the official records and personal or private papers in all depositories; the compilation of a bibliography of the publications that resulted from the expeditions and programs before 1942; and reference service to qualified researchers on material in its custody. The National Archives is following the best traditions of Kane "to preserve the documents of the Expedition."

It is, of course, a truism that to gather and preserve all of the official records and personal papers in an optimum environment is in itself important. But these documents are of little value unless they can ultimately be identified, described, and used in the interest of scholarship. We will explore every approach that promises greater facility in the use of these materials. Ultimately, computerized methods of information retrieval may be applied to such holdings; a long-term study of such a possibility has been started in the National Archives. Of course each body of personal papers given in the name of or by a person will retain its identity as a separate collection, and any restrictions placed by the donor on its use will be observed.

We invite your interest and your participation.

We are indeed fortunate in having as our speakers today men and women who have given much of their time over many years to polar fieldwork and research. They have kindly consented to address us on a variety of subjects pertaining to the history of geographical exploration and of science in the polar regions.

SESSION I
Highlights of United States Exploration and Research in the Arctic

CHAIRMAN:

Louis O. Quam

Appointed Chief Scientist for the Antarctic Programs Office, National Science Foundation, in September, 1967, Dr. Quam was a university professor before and after serving in the Navy during World War II. From 1950 until his recent appointment, he was with the Office of Naval Research.

The first session begins with two papers that together give the highlights of the long history of U.S. scientific exploration and research in the Arctic. Those of us who are aware of the history can only conclude that our speakers have a herculean task in compacting so much information into the short time allotted them. These papers will be followed by comments from several authorities in very special kinds of activities that herald the full use of modern science in polar exploration.

UNITED STATES ARCTIC EXPLORATION THROUGH 1939

Walter A. Wood

Leader of the American Geographic Society Yukon Expeditions, the McCall Glacier Project of IGY, 1957-58, and of the Icefield Ranges Research Programs in Alaska, Dr. Wood has also served on and directed numerous expeditions in the Arctic; has held responsible positions in the American Geographical Society, the Arctic Institute of North America, and the Explorer's Club; and has published extensively in professional journals.

When one finds the words "arctic" and "exploration" in the title of a program, it is well, I think, to begin with definitions; and here a speaker can presumably be allowed some license in selecting the boundaries of area and of meaning that he interprets as encompassing the purpose at hand. This morning, and in this setting, I have chosen to interpret "arctic" rather liberally and "exploration" according to the rather refined meaning given by the dictionary.

Having an affectionate regard for the Arctic Institute of North America and its works, I choose to define "arctic" as the region encompassed by the *Arctic Bibliography* compiled and published by the institute. Those of you who are familiar with this essential research tool will immediately recognize that, at least as far as the North American Arctic is concerned, I have accepted the word in its broadest meaning. This is borne out by my having been told by Marie Tremaine, the devoted editor of the *Arctic Bibliography,* that it contains some 8,300 entries under "exploration." If I am to do a thorough job, will you settle back in your seats while I start with "Exploration-Anthropology" and work through to "Exploration-Zoology" in the next two and a half hours—with fervent apologies to those scheduled to follow me on this platform!

Happily, you are to be spared such an ordeal by circumstances, the most important of which is the word "highlights" in the program title, and that will endear me to you by several thousand items. Then, too, we are concerned today only with the part played by the United States, its citizens and institutions, in arctic exploration. This fact again reduces the subject matter both geographically and historically. I choose to define "exploration" as the process of adding to human knowledge through geographical observation, interpretation, and reporting.

Even by narrowing our terms of reference as I have suggested, there remain more than two hundred exploratory programs organized and carried out under U.S. aegis between 1776 and 1939. The best I can hope to do is to be brutally selective, perhaps thereby alienating myself from many of you who may not be sympathetic to my emphasis and perhaps seeming discourteous to a legion of highly distinguished efforts that have made lasting places for themselves in U.S. arctic history.

It is interesting to note that the signing of the Declaration of Independence was no signal for the United States to jump promptly and with energy into the arctic arena. In fact, with one exception, over seventy years were to pass before there was organized U.S. interest in the Arctic. That exception is an interesting one. In 1789 John Churchman first sought assistance from the Government to commence the delineation of the unknown and frozen lands of the Far North. Like so many men after him, Churchman was turned down. It was only in 1848 that whaling captain James Royce on the *Superior* first carried the Stars and Stripes through the waters of Bering Strait and into the Arctic Ocean.

How often it happens that tragedy is the spark that ignites discovery and speeds understanding of little-known areas. It was tragedy that opened the doors to U.S. arctic history. Had not Sir John Franklin and 129 men become overdue in 1847 while seeking to link the sealanes of the Atlantic and the Pacific via the Northwest Passage, one can suggest that serious interest in the Arctic might have been delayed at least until the purchase of Alaska in 1867. Franklin's disappearance set in motion perhaps the most intensive search in history, and to that search the United States responded with its first entries into arctic exploration.

Between 1850 and 1873 four men wrote classic chapters of U.S. arctic history. They were Lieutenant Edwin De Haven, Elisha Kent Kane, Isaac Israel Hayes, and Charles Francis Hall. All of them found sponsorship and financing from leading institutions, notably the Smithsonian Institution, the American Philosophical Society, and the American Geographical Society. All found assistance from the U.S. Navy.

In those years much was added to the world's sum of geographical knowledge, particularly of the lands, channels, and passages that we now loosely call the Eastern Canadian Arctic and the west coast of Greenland. At the same time much was learned of arctic travel and living. The techniques of Kane became the practices of Robert E. Peary, and the adoption of the Eskimo way of life was later to find full impact through the clear voice of Vilhjalmur Stefansson.

As fragments of evidence from many sources—Hall was a notable contributor—conclusively proved that disaster had overtaken Franklin and his men, emphasis shifted from search to exploration toward the North Pole; but before it could swing into high gear there occurred one of the true highlights of arctic—indeed of polar—chronology.

In 1879 at a meeting in Hamburg, eleven nations pledged a one-year manning, in 1882-83, of polar stations; at each of these stations an identical series of scientific observations would be carried out simultaneously and continuously. To this network the United States contributed two: one at Point Barrow, Alaska, under Lieutenant Patrick H. Ray, and the other at Lady Franklin Bay on the northeast coast of Ellesmere Island under Lieutenant Adolphus W. Greely. Thus there came into being the first attempt, and a most successful one, at international cooperation in polar science. So successful, indeed, was the first international polar year that it gave rise to a second in 1932-33 and to the International Geophysical Year still fresh in our recent past.

While the programs of Ray and Greely were identical, there the similarity of the two efforts ended. Point Barrow was then well known to whalers, and Ray had little difficulty in reaching it or in carrying out his appointed tasks. He did little traveling from his base, and his party was well supplied and safely evacuated. In contrast, Greely's base at Fort Conger was difficult to reach, and resupply of it was unpredictable. Although interdisciplinary studies were carried out, much of the data was subsequently lost. Geographical knowledge was expanded primarily through the fine journeys of Greely into the interior of Ellesmere Island and through Lieutenant J. B. Lockwood's long sledging trip along the north coast of Greenland and his traverse across Ellesmere Island to Greely Fiord. Then disaster struck. Greely was not resupplied in 1882. In 1883 he augmented his dwindling stores with several extremely small caches that were found as his party retreated south from Fort Conger. When help came in June, 1884, only seven men remained alive out of the twenty-five who had made up the expedition party.

Now the route to the Arctic Ocean and to the pole had been charted, but before it was used another epic tragedy was recorded. There were those who believed that Bering Strait was the gateway to the pole, and their belief was based on what we know today to have been two fallacious theories. The first was that the warm Japanese Current contributed to an ice-free polar sea; the second was that a land mass, the coast of which could be followed northward, projected far into the Asiatic quadrant.

In 1879 Lieutenant George Washington DeLong sailed the *Jeannette* north from San Francisco and boldly took her into the pack ice near Herald Island. But the ice failed to loosen, and for nearly two years the *Jeannette* drifted with the winds and currents until she was crushed north of the New Siberian Islands. After traveling over ice and open seas, part of the ship's company reached the delta of the Lena River in two parties (another part of the crew was lost and never heard from). One party, led by Lieutenant George W. Melville, encountered a native and was led to safety; all but two men of the other party, led by DeLong, weakened and died within a score of miles of rescue.

From the disaster of the *Jeannette* came much of scientific importance. In terms of effect on arctic exploration, the most significant result was the mapping of a primary current of the Arctic Ocean. It was this evidence that was to be of crucial importance to the plans of Fridtjof Nansen and the drift of the *Fram* twelve years later.

Probably there is no schoolchild in this country who has not been taught that in 1909 Robert E. Peary reached the North Pole. Not all have learned, though, of the thirteen years of obsession, dedication, endurance, and willpower that got him there. Nor can I in the minutes available this morning do more than remind you of eight separate expeditions and nine winters in the Arctic; of three journeys across the Greenland icecap and the first tracing of the north coast of Greenland; of trips into the interior of Ellesmere Island and along its northern coast to Axel Heiberg Island; and finally of the three successively deeper penetrations of the frozen Arctic Ocean that enabled him to report to the Secretary of State that he had "hoisted [the] stars and stripes on [the] north pole."[1] If you would know more of Peary the man or of what he did, I urge you to read—not his book *The North Pole,* written under the glare of the public spotlight, in trains and hotel rooms while on lecture trips— but rather his detailed reports that appeared in the *Bulletin* of the American Geographical Society, of which he was president during so many of the years of crescendo that led to final victory.

Of Frederick A. Cook let me merely suggest that it is no longer important whether or not he reached the pole. Bitterness, hate, and invective have been spared others in polar history whose behavior was no better than Cook's was alleged to be. Perhaps it is more charitable to remember that in circuiting Ellesmere and Axel Heiberg Islands he performed a very considerable journey of over 1,000 miles. But if some insist that history must be served, let them remember that the more we come to understand the physical geography of the Arctic Ocean the more we recognize phenomena described by Cook but unknown at the time of his journey.

Coinciding with the Peary era were seven U.S. organized and financed expeditions into the European quadrant of the Arctic. The impetus came from Walter Wellman who, with the attainment of the pole in mind, led five of the forays—four of them based on Spitsbergen. The others, outgrowths of Wellman's incentive, were led by Evelyn Briggs Baldwin and Anthony Fiala and centered on the archipelago of Franz Josef Land. So far as progress toward the pole is concerned, none of these expeditions went very far. Scientifically, much was accomplished and published. Also on the positive side was Well-

---

[1] Telegram from Robert E. Peary to the Secretary of State, September 10, 1909, numerical file 14943/1, Record Group 59, General Records of the Department of State, National Archives.

man's vision that foresaw the use of mechanized vehicles for arctic travel and the actual use of the first powered aircraft—an airship—to attempt to reach the pole.

Thus far I have put the spotlight on what might be called the great classic expeditions in the grand tradition. All of them had two things in common: the attainment of the North Pole was, to some degree at least, involved in each; and they all attracted wide national interest. Also, perhaps none was free of the frictions that so easily beset enterprises in a hostile environment. Not necessarily common to all was the advancement of scientific knowledge.

It is well to remember that for each of these great classics of exploration there were, even before World War I, perhaps a dozen expeditions, large and small, that deserve spotlights of at least equal candlepower. Almost all of them had to do with the unveiling and subsequent development of Alaska.

Just as the English passed on to us basic knowledge of the high North American Arctic, so the Russians gave us a headstart in understanding Alaska. In 1867 much of coastal Alaska was known and the major features of the interior vaguely understood. But at the time of purchase, and for some thirty-five years after it, basic exploration was performed by candidates for a hall of fame second to none in history. To make the record even more impressive, the map was unrolled by men who represented a variety of Government agencies and who had little official support. "For many years . . . the United States Government made no systematic effort to explore the interior. Such official explorations as were made were largely due to the initiative of some Government employees, and often received but scant support, and in some cases even open opposition, from the authorities at Washington. It is, therefore, to the greatest credit of these early explorers that they carried out difficult projects with but little help and with no hope of any official recognition of their efforts."[2]

Who were some of these men? Robert Kennicott; George Davidson and William H. Dall of the Coast and Geodetic Survey; Captain Charles W. Raymond of the Army and his service colleague, the extraordinary Frederick Schwatka, who, fresh from leading the last of the classic searches for Franklin, conducted a brilliant survey of the Yukon River Basin from its source in Yukon Territory to the

[2] Alfred H. Brooks, *Blazing Alaska's Trails* (University of Alaska and the Arctic Institute of North America, 1953), p. 272.

Bering Sea—without, I might add, the sanction of the War Department. Then came Lieutenant Henry T. Allen's great journey up the Copper River, across the Alaska Range, and down the Yukon to the sea.

I have mentioned the work of Ray at Point Barrow during the first polar year, and to it must be added the three seasons of Lieutenant George M. Stoney in northwestern Alaska between 1883 and 1885 that stand as classics in the exploration of that region. And so it went: men like Alfred H. Brooks, Walter C. Mendenhall, Fred H. Moffit, Ernest de Koven Leffingwell, and Philip S. Smith—all of the Geological Survey; the semi-anonymous titans of the international boundary surveys; and the men of the Navy and the Revenue Cutter Service. The list could go on. They were joined, too, by the independent scientific community, well represented by the unique Harriman expedition of 1899 and the work of Ralph S. Tarr and Lawrence Martin for the National Geographic Society ten years later—and all to the end of assembling a composite picture of Alaska, a picture to which brush strokes are still being added today.

Even as Peary was sailing north on his final journey, a new star was rising on the polar scene. His name was Vilhjalmur Stefansson. From 1906 when he joined Einar Mikkelsen and Leffingwell in the Beaufort Sea to his death only a few years ago, he compiled a record as explorer, scientist, historian, prophet, and symbol of the Arctic that is unequalled. The sixteen volumes of the Canadian Arctic Expedition of 1913-18, which he commanded, stand alone to this day as the single most valuable scientific contribution to our knowledge of Arctic North America ever compiled. They assemble the record of the last of the classic U.S. polar expeditions, unless, of course, we wish to classify Admiral Donald B. MacMillan's journeys as expeditions. And, indeed, we might well do so, since from 1908, nearly sixty years ago, the eastern Arctic has been his life and his almost annual stamping ground. But MacMillan did one thing that Stefansson did not do. He used the third dimension of exploration—the airplane—to assist him.

And so we come to the air age and a whole new era in exploration. It began with Salomon A. Andrée and then with Wellman. In 1925 there rocketed to prominence two American names that were destined to be as lasting as any in U.S. polar history: Richard E. Byrd and Lincoln Ellsworth.

As though it had never been reached, the North Pole again became a magnet. While Byrd was flying with MacMillan over Ellesmere Island and Greenland in 1925, Ellsworth joined Roald Amundsen in a venture toward the pole that penetrated to within 130 miles of its objective and escaped disaster by a near miracle. The following year Byrd, with Floyd Bennett as pilot, entered the polar race. From Kings Bay, Spitsbergen, on May 9, 1926, they took off, and in a flight of about eight hours reached the pole. Scarcely had they returned victorious to Spitsbergen than Ellsworth, Amundsen, and Umberto Nobile with a crew of fourteen, including one dog, set out in the airship *N-1* to repeat the flight and to continue across the Arctic Ocean to Alaska. They were completely successful and, in a flight of nearly three days, accomplished the first transit of the Arctic Basin.

Meanwhile, another man of vision was adapting the airplane to the needs of polar exploration. George Hubert Wilkins, an Australian by birth, as a boy had yearned to follow the antarctic trails of Amundsen, Sir Ernest Shackleton, and Robert F. Scott. In 1912 Wilkins received a telegram inviting him to come to London to join a polar expedition, and, assuming his dream to have come true, he accepted—only to find that he had been signed on by Stefansson for the Canadian Arctic Expedition. Thus he became one of us.

In 1926 and 1927 Wilkins and Ben Eielson blazed pioneer trails from Alaska out over the Arctic Ocean, making landings, both forced and intentional, in the interests of scientific observation. It was in 1928 that the pair made their greatest flight. Byrd and Ellsworth had followed meridian courses to their objectives, thus simplifying navigation. Wilkins chose new techniques developed for him by the American Geographical Society and boldly took off across the Arctic Ocean on a course toward Spitsbergen that would permit him, hopefully, to determine whether lands existed north of Ellesmere Island as reported by Peary and by Cook. The flight was an operational success of 2,200 miles, but poor visibility obscured the critical area. It was only in 1946 that aerial reconnaissance eliminated Crocker Land and Bradley Land as geographical proper names.

It is well to bring the pre-World War II period to an end with Wilkins, for in the Arctic he was one of the staunch bridges between the old and the modern eras of exploration. It was he who echoed Stefansson in calling for an increased understanding of the polar Mediterranean. It was he who dreamed of a polar community of weather stations. And it was he who first demonstrated the use of the submarine in polar waters, thus anticipating the present value of the nuclear submarine in the Arctic.

Time is short, and the remaining highlights are still legion. Many of you in this hall richly merit to be singled out, for in the 1920s and 1930s you set the pace for a new era of increased, inter-disciplinary scientific progress. Your reward today must be the satisfaction of having played a part in the often-quoted sequitur, "The past is the key to the present." It is a present that you have shared in bringing about and one to which only such a man as John Reed can bring us this morning.

UNITED STATES ARCTIC EXPLORATION
SINCE 1939

John C. Reed

Executive Director of the Arctic Institute of North America
since 1961, Dr. Reed was a geologist and an administrator
with the U.S. Geological Survey from 1930 to 1961 except
for his service with the U.S. Navy during World War II. He
has done fieldwork in Alaska and is the author of a number
of definitive studies on ore deposits in Alaska. [Dr. Reed
retired as Executive Director of the Arctic Institute of
North America and became the Institute Senior Scientist
on January 1, 1968.]

*This day of review and discussion of U.S. exploration and research in
the polar regions, so kindly provided by the National Archives,
seems especially appropriate in 1967—a centennial year for all parts
of North America that border the north polar ocean, except, of
course, for Greenland. Canada's fabulous Expo-67, commemorating
the centennial of its confederation, includes under the main subject,
"Man and His World," the major theme, "Man the Explorer," and
the subtheme, "Man and the Polar Regions."*

*Walter Wood has masterfully carried the story of U.S. arctic ex-
ploration up to 1939, and he is a hard man to follow in the speaker's
platform. I must try to treat U.S. arctic exploration and research
since 1939 in only twenty minutes. It is, of course, completely impossible to do the story justice in anything like that amount of time.
I will not be able to say anything detailed about the attainment of
statehood by Alaska, which has had a positive and exemplary effect
on research and exploration in our forty-ninth State. For the most*

part, I will leave out specific mention of the constructive and influential research conducted by a number of "old line" Federal agencies for many, many years—the Weather Bureau, the Geological Survey, the Bureau of Mines, the Coast and Geodetic Survey, and others. I will have to skip over projects such as the Icefield Ranges Research Project of the Arctic Institute of North America and the American Geographical Society; Camps Century and Tuto of the U.S. Army in Greenland; Project Blue Ice of the Arctic Institute, sponsored by the U.S. Air Force Office of Scientific Research; and the Juneau Icefield Research Project of Michigan State University, headed by Maynard M. Miller. These omissions I regret, but they are necessary.

Some of us whose responsibilities include finding financial support for arctic research from governments, industry, foundations, and private individuals soon develop the habit of emphasizing the small amount of arctic research that has gone on and is going on. Some informed people believe that much more U.S. arctic research is desirable and fully justified. Nevertheless, in the past thirty years a lot has gone on; a surprising advance has been made in what we know about the Arctic and how to operate there. The subjects to which I plan to give specific attention were selected because I feel they are especially significant in the buildup of this body of useful information.

NAVAL PETROLEUM RESERVE NO. 4
and
THE ARCTIC RESEARCH LABORATORY

On a cold, windy, drizzly day in August, 1944, a gray-hulled Navy ship appeared through the scud off the long sandy beach that projects into the Arctic Ocean to form Point Barrow, the northernmost point of Alaska [fig. 1]. A boat was lowered and moved ashore. From it stepped Lieutenant Commander W. H. Rex, fresh from a Seabee detachment in the Aleutians, to greet Lieutenant W. T. Foran, geologist and head of a small advance geologic and planning party. Thus began the exploration for oil in the 70,000 square miles or so of tundra-covered plains and foothills that stretch from the Arctic coast to the jagged Brooks Range—including the area designated as Naval

FIGURE 1—The view northward along Point Barrow beach during the activity of Naval Petroleum Reserve No. 4.

Petroleum Reserve No. 4 (PET 4) by President Harding in 1923. Ten years and about $55 million later, many of the details of that large area had been studied, interpreted, and recorded. Complete aerial photocoverage had been obtained, excellent maps had been made, the areal and structural geology had been investigated, exploration holes had been drilled, a medium-sized oilfield had been found and its potential partially determined, and several gasfields of great potential significance had been identified. Over the tundra for all those years churned the Weasels of field parties during the summers, and great tractor trains loaded with all manner of oilfield equipment and supplies roared over the frozen surface during the long dark winters. In the process, a body of knowledge was accumulated about environment and logistics over land and sea and in the air that was unique in the experience of the United States. Outstanding in the whole PET 4 operation, which was terminated in 1953, was Commodore William G. Greenman. It was his faith, energy, and ability that resulted in PET 4 and kept it going for several discouraging years before success was attained.

Piggyback on PET 4, and beginning in August, 1947, came the Arctic Research Laboratory (ARL)[1] of the Office of Naval Research (ONR). A contract operation from the start, ARL has been operated by Swarthmore College, Johns Hopkins University, and the University of Alaska in that order. From the laboratory in the old PET 4 camp at Point Barrow, about fifteen hundred researchers in many disciplines and from many universities have scattered far and wide over the tundra and out to sea—including riding huge ice cakes around and around the Arctic Ocean. ARL has continued up to the present and is one of the principal facilities at Point Barrow. A new and more modern laboratory is now under construction.

ARL's record of productive research is enviable indeed, and the opportunities ahead seem even greater. The ONR and the universities that have participated should be proud of their achievement. The following distinguished directors have guided ARL along its sometimes difficult path: Laurence Irving, George E. MacGinitie, Ira L. Wiggins, Ted C. Mathews, G. Dallas Hanna, and, currently, Max C. Brewer. Supporting them all the way from ONR headquarters in Washington have been other dedicated scientists performing the fundamentally necessary functions of planning, budgeting, and justifying the field operations. I cannot be exhaustive in mentioning names, but among them are M. C. Shelesnyak, John Field, Louis O. Quam, and Max E. Britton.

PET 4 and its longer-lived companion, ARL, constitute an epic chapter in U.S. arctic exploration.

Project Chariot

In 1826, working northeast from Bering Strait, H.M.S. *Blossom*, Captain F. W. Beechey in command, rounded what he described as "a high cape, which I named after Mr. Deas Thomson, one of the

---

[1] Recently the Arctic Research Laboratory was renamed the Naval Arctic Research Laboratory. The earlier name is used throughout this paper.

commissioners of the navy."[2] Thus was named the remote cape of northwestern Alaska that between 1959 and 1961 was thoroughly explored in all its environmental aspects. The exploring investigations were known as *Project Chariot,* and it was part of the *Plowshare Program*—the study of the peaceful uses of nuclear explosives. The purpose of *Chariot* was to appraise the effects of excavating a harbor by nuclear explosions. To do this, there had to be factual information derived from exhaustive investigations of the environment before the explosions. The investigations that were carried out by almost a hundred scientists led to a comprehensive understanding of that stretch of bleak tundra. The results were reported in detail.[3]

In 1962 *Chariot* was suspended and no explosives were detonated. Many predictions would have been tested and many questions would have been answered if the explosions had taken place and the environment subsequently studied again. Nevertheless, the project stands as an illustration of what can be done through a comprehensive study of a selected site.

THE UNIVERSITY OF ALASKA

On a spruce- and birch-covered hill a few miles west of Fairbanks, Alaska, on a hot summer day in 1915, a little group gathered to lay the cornerstone of a small land-grant college in a ceremony led by Judge James Wickersham, Delegate to Congress from the Territory of Alaska. For a long time it was a pretty small center of higher education in a big, big wilderness. At times the road was rough and rocky, but the first president, Charles E. Bunnell, never faltered in his determination to develop a real university. After World War II, substantial growth began. In 1949 the second president was installed—Terris Moore, educator, philosopher, accomplished light-aircraft pilot, and famed mountaineer. He was followed in 1953 by Ernest N. Patty, successful mining engineer and former dean of the university's School of Mines; and he in 1960 by William Wood, un-

[2] Donald J. Orth, *Dictionary of Alaska Place Names,* Geological Survey Professional Paper 567 (Washington, 1967), p. 961. According to Orth, "Beechey spelled the name 'Thompson' on his chart, a form that has been copied by succeeding cartographers."

[3] N. J. Wilimovsky and J. N. Wolfe (eds.), *Environment of the Cape Thompson Region, Alaska* (Oak Ridge, 1966).

der whose regime the university has attained its present status of statewide and national importance.

From the start a few faculty members had engaged in exploration of various types, but the effort was small and not of great significance in some fields. In 1946 a bill sponsored by E. L. Bartlett, then Delegate to Congress from the Territory of Alaska, was passed by Congress authorizing the establishment at the university of the Geophysical Institute. A few years later the Geophysical Institute became an integral part of the university and soon earned recognition in the broad field of geophysics, especially in studies of the upper atmosphere and ionosphere.

Following the Geophysical Institute, which now is planning a new and much more adequate building, a series of institutes came into being. I am confident that more will be established as time goes on. Each is designed for research, which really is exploration, in segments of interest of special pertinency to Alaska. Already there are an Institute of Arctic Biology, an Institute of Marine Sciences, and an Institute of Social, Economic, and Government Research. Progress is being made, and many problems of intriguing interest await attention.

Exploration in the form of research is being advanced on many fronts by the institutes mentioned and by the regular departments of the university. Increasingly, Federal agencies and others interested in various aspects of Alaskan development are turning to the university for help. Meetings and symposia, such as the International Conference on Polar Bears in 1966 and the International Symposium of Circumpolar Health-Related Problems in 1967, are being held at the university. As has been pointed out, ARL at Point Barrow is now operated by the university under contract with ONR.

JOINT ARCTIC WEATHER STATIONS

Weather is always with us, and this is just as true of the Arctic as it is right here in the District of Columbia, although usually with a little different emphasis. Weather Bureau officials, along with their counterparts in Canada and in Denmark for Greenland, have tried to do something about it in the Arctic. They created JAWS—the

Joint Arctic Weather Stations. The story is fascinating, and I regret that I can give it only the briefest attention.

In order to support the postwar increase in transatlantic air travel and possible future transpolar flights, the United States, Canada, and Denmark decided in 1946 to establish a chain of weather stations in Arctic Canada and Greenland. Under the guidance of Lieutenant Colonel Charles J. Hubbard, JAWS became a reality. Tragically, Colonel Hubbard was killed in the crash of a Royal Canadian Air Force plane along with eight Canadian companions during the construction of Alert in 1950. All nine are buried at Alert on a point overlooking the Arctic Ocean.

The only station established in Greenland as part of JAWS was Thule. It subsequently was taken over by the U.S. Military Establishment and separated from JAWS.

JAWS today is composed of five stations maintained and operated jointly by Canada and the United States. The network was established in the late 1940's and early 1950's. Eureka was the first, established in 1947 on the western side of Ellesmere Island. Transportation was by the U.S. Air Force operating out of Thule, Greenland. Mould Bay and Isachsen were set up in the spring of 1948 on Prince Patrick Island and Ellef Ringnes Island, respectively. In the summer of 1948 vessels of the U.S. Navy established Resolute on Cornwallis Island. This became the main supply and operating base. Alert was the last to be established, in 1950, at the northern tip of Ellesmere Island by aircraft of the U.S. Air Force operating out of Thule.

In 1961 the first nuclear-powered automatic weather station was installed on Axel Heiberg Island under the direction of J. Glen Dyer of the U.S. Weather Bureau and Donald C. Archibald of the Canadian Meteorological Service. Although this station was established under the JAWS agreement, it was experimental only and was not considered a regular JAWS station. It has been discontinued.

THE INTERNATIONAL GEOPHYSICAL YEAR

In 1882-83, at the time of the first international polar year, the need for geophysical data in the study of man's physical environment was recognized. However, as Lieutenant Patrick H. Ray, U.S. Army, carried out the work of that first polar year at Point Barrow, I doubt that he had any idea of the chain of events that would follow. Fifty years later came the second polar year, and in 1957 occurred the really big one—the International Geophysical Year (IGY) that was 18 months long, from July 1, 1957, to December 31, 1958.

United States efforts during IGY included substantial activity in the Arctic as well as in many other places. "The U.S. participated in scientific studies at a total of 76 arctic stations. Thirty-seven were in cooperation with other nations: Canada, Sweden, Denmark, Iceland, Norway, and the UK [sic]."[4] Two major scientific stations were operated on floating ice in the Arctic Ocean. In addition, stations were established on the McCall Glacier in the Brooks Range, Alaska, and on the Blue Glacier in the Olympic Mountains, Washington, for special glaciological studies. Scientific studies were carried out in aurora and airglow, cosmic rays, geomagnetism, glaciology, gravity, ionospheric physics, meteorology, nuclear radiation, oceanography, rocketry, and seismology. This was a substantial and productive effort, and the United States can justly take pride in its accomplishments.

NUCLEAR SUBMARINES

It was late in July, 1958; the sleek, dark hull of the nuclear-powered submarine U.S.S. *Nautilus,* Captain William R. Anderson in command, slipped quietly out of Pearl Harbor, Hawaii, and set a course northward, once in the open sea. Thus began the first transit of the Arctic Ocean by nuclear submarine. In 96 hours the *Nautilus* crossed the Arctic Ocean at high speed beneath the ice without once surfacing between Point Barrow and Spitsbergen.

Since 1931, when Sir Hubert Wilkins first took a submarine under the polar ice, ships, instruments, and techniques have been improved to the point that, "The Arctic Ocean has become the private sea of the submariner who is free to move in any direction and at any speed under the ice covering the sea."[5] In March, 1959, the

[4] National Academy of Sciences, Geophysics Research Board, *Report on the U.S. Program for the International Geophysical Year, July 1, 1957–December 31, 1958,* IGY General Report No. 21 (Washington, 1965) , p. 837.

[5] Waldo Lyon, "The Submarine and the Arctic Ocean," *Polar Record,* II (September, 1963) , 699.

Skate cruised under the Arctic Ocean and proved the feasibility of surfacing through the winter ice. In February, 1960, the *Sargo* entered the Arctic Basin through more than 1,000 miles of shallow water where ridges of ice penetrated so deep that the submarine had to maneuver around them to avoid collision. Yet 20 successful surfacings were made in 30 days during the midwinter polar darkness. In the summer of that year the *Seadragon* made the first east-west transit, traveling through Baffin Bay (infested with deep-draft icebergs), Lancaster Sound, Viscount Melville Sound, and M'Clure Strait into the Beaufort Sea. In 1962 the *Skate* (out of New London, Connecticut) and the *Seadragon* (out of Pearl Harbor, Hawaii) proceeded from opposite sides of the earth into the Arctic Ocean and rendezvoused beneath the ice at a prearranged point and a prearranged time on July 31. They then proceeded together to the Beaufort Sea, where they conducted joint operations with the icebreaker U.S.S. *Staten Island.*

The scientific results of those voyages have been great indeed, and the achievements will long be remembered.

FLOATING STATIONS

Around the Arctic Ocean, at the whim of wind and current, drift huge islands of ice many tens of feet in thickness and of areal extent like the District of Columbia. We know where these ghostly wanderers in the arctic pack come from, but, almost inconceivably, we do not know how many there are, where most of them are, or how long they last. The story of their discovery by Americans (they well may have been recognized earlier by our Soviet colleagues) and their subsequent use as research platforms is a saga of U.S. exploration carried out on a shoestring with most noteworthy results.

In 1949 planes of the U.S. Air Force Air Weather Service, droning back and forth between Ladd or Eielson Air Force Bases in central Alaska and the North Pole to observe weather and sea ice conditions, discovered some of those king-size ice cubes. The radar observers wondered about them. In 1952 Lieutenant Colonel Joseph O. Fletcher, U.S. Air Force, established a scientific station on one of them, then at 87°54′ N., 165°30′ W. That particular platform has since had a long, but somewhat sporadic, history of U.S. occu-

pancy. Soon it became known popularly as T-3 and, even more appropriately, as Fletcher's Ice Island.

Fletcher's Ice Island was occupied from 1952 to May, 1954. It
was reoccupied from April to September, 1955. In March and April,
1957, the Alaskan Air Command established two drifting stations for
the U.S. IGY program—Station ALPHA on sea ice at 79°40′ N.,
159° W., and Station BRAVO on Fletcher's Ice Island then at
82°46′ N., 99°33′ W. This was the famed *Project Ice Skate*. ALPHA
was breaking up and was therefore evacuated in early November,
1958. BRAVO, on the more resistant ice island, was occupied until
October, 1961, even though it had been aground and stationary at
71°52′ N., 160°20′ W., since July, 1960. In lieu of ALPHA, the Office
of Naval Research and the Alaskan Air Command established Station CHARLIE, often called ALPHA II, at the end of April, 1959.
It had to be abandoned in January, 1960, because of the breaking up
of the floe—a very short life.

During the time I have just been discussing largely in terms of
Air Force activity, the Navy was also getting into the business of
research from floating stations. Its record is a fascinating one of determination and initiative in the face of all sorts of discouragement
and disappointment. The Navy, in addition to long-term interest,
had two specific, rather short-range objectives—to develop methods
of forecasting sea ice conditions to aid ships dispatched annually to
resupply the PET 4 operation and to explore the Arctic Basin's potential use by nuclear submarines. In 1951 the Navy mounted *Project
Ski Jump I* by an R4D aircraft operating out of Point Barrow. Three
oceanographic stations were established on the sea ice. In 1952 the
project was expanded, and the R4D was supported by P2V aircraft.
This was *Project Ski Jump II*. Near the end of March, 1952, the
landing gear of the R4D collapsed while taking off from a remote
station on the ice, and both aircraft and equipment had to be abandoned.

Then came the famed ARLIS stations (named for Arctic Research Laboratory Ice Station). The concept was to keep the logistics
simple and inexpensive. Generally R4D's and Cessna-180's from
Point Barrow were used as support aircraft; icebreakers were utilized
for support when possible. ARLIS I was set on an ice floe in September, 1960, and a small group of scientists and support personnel rode
it until mid-March, 1961, when it was evacuated because it was drift-

ing too far west. Then came ARLIS II with probably the most colorful history of all. It was established on an accidentally found ice island in May, 1961, and was occupied continuously for 4 years. In that time it drifted more than 4,300 nautical miles and was evacuated by the icebreaker *Edisto* in May, 1965, in the Denmark Strait between Iceland and Greenland. During those 4 years more than 100 scientists had carried out research at the station.

For a large part of the time that ARLIS II was occupied, Fletcher's Ice Island drifted in a remarkably fortunate course relative to it and to the Arctic Research Laboratory at Point Barrow. Fletcher's Ice Island generally lay between the two and provided a necessary intermediate point for refueling the R4D. The last R4D flight to carry supplies from Point Barrow flew about 18 hours to reach ARLIS II, stopping at Fletcher's Ice Island and at Alert. The next day the plane went on from ARLIS II to Keflavik, Iceland, which it reached in less than 4 hours.

Since the time of ARLIS II, the Office of Naval Research has continued to support research on floating stations, mostly on Fletcher's Ice Island. But several other ARLIS stations have been established and briefly occupied on other ice islands.

SUMMARY

We have seen that modern arctic exploration has many faces, and through them all runs the common determination to extend the frontiers of knowledge and therefore man's appreciation of the environment in which he lives. With the continuation of this determination, think of the potential of the new Arctic Research laboratory now under construction and of the possibilities of the present and the yet-to-be-formed research institutes of the University of Alaska! Consider what may derive from our ever-increasing ability to sense all manner of terrain features and even animals from high-flying aircraft and from satellites! Speculate on the vistas that may open through our search for scientific facts and for resources on the continental shelves and in the ocean depths! The future of arctic exploration is more intriguing and exciting than ever. The future begins now!

COMMENTS ON THE VOYAGE OF THE U.S.S. *NAUTILUS*

William R. Anderson

READ BY LOUIS O. QUAM

A graduate of the U.S. Naval Academy in 1942, Representative Anderson remained on active duty with the Navy until 1962, serving as commander of the atomic submarine *Nautilus,* 1957-59, and as assistant to Vice Adm. H. G. Rickover and Secretaries of the Navy William B. Franke, John Connally, and Fred Korth, 1959-62. In 1964 he was elected to Congress from the Sixth District of Tennessee.

I am extremely sorry that the press of congressional business in my district incident to the Labor Day recess prevents my being present on this excellent occasion.

Through the assistance of Vice Admiral Rickover, and through his own gracious acceptance, it has been possible to arrange for my navigator on the Nautilus *to be with you and to deliver a brief paper. He is Commander Shepherd M. Jenks, now Commanding Officer of the U.S. Naval Nuclear Power Training Unit at West Milton, New York.*

Vilhjalmur Stefansson, more than three decades before the first nuclear submarine thrust under the polar ice, predicted that the true agent of commerce in the Arctic would be the submarine. Sir Hubert Wilkins believed in the principle but failed in practice because his submarine was inadequate.

Nuclear power has opened up a new dimension in the Arctic— the dimension underneath the ice. In 1958 the Nautilus *voyage helped restore a sputnik-shaken United States. More importantly in the long run, it helped to show the Arctic as it truly is—a huge ocean, often 2 or more miles deep, capped by a relatively modest layer of ice.*

There is no question but that Stefansson's prediction will come true.

In years to come large cargo-carrying submarines will be built. Such submarines will ply between the Far East and Europe via the pole, cutting the sea distance almost in half. They may also constitute a feasible means of bringing out the rich mineral reserve from northern Canada and other parts of the Arctic.

The submarine is an immensely valuable means of collecting scientific data in the Arctic. With it, it is relatively easy to complete a detailed mapping of the ocean floor. Nor should the military value of it in the Arctic Ocean be overlooked—whether in terms of the missile submarine or perhaps the antiballistic-missile submarine.

It is inconceivable that man will fail to utilize vigorously and fully an ocean five times the size of the Mediterranean Sea now that he possesses the essential tools to do so.

OPERATION SUNSHINE: THE TRANSPOLAR VOYAGE OF THE U.S.S. NAUTILUS BENEATH THE ICE OF THE ARCTIC BASIN, AUGUST, 1958

Shepherd M. Jenks

Commanding Officer of the Nuclear Power Training Unit since 1964, Commander Jenks graduated from the U.S. Naval Academy in 1949 and began his special training in nuclear power in 1954. He was the navigator of the atomic submarine *Nautilus* during its historic transect of the Arctic Ocean in 1958.

On August 5, 1958, the U.S.S. *Nautilus* surfaced in the Greenland Sea and sent two messages: "Nautilus 90 North"[1] and "Ninety-six Hours, Point Barrow to the Greenland Sea."[2] In the previous 4 days she had steamed 1,839 miles under the arctic ice; had become the first ship in history to attain the North Pole; and, with 116 men on board, had proved that a transpolar passage, by sea, between the Pacific and Atlantic Oceans was possible.

It had been exactly one year since Captain William R. Anderson, leaving the *Nautilus* at the Electric Boat Company piers in Groton, Connecticut, had flown over the ice pack for on-the-spot observations before the first penetration under the ice by a nuclear submarine. It had been planned that en route to a NATO exercise

---

[1] William R. Anderson, with Clay Blair, Jr., *Nautilus 90 North* (Cleveland, 1959), p. 234.

[2] *Ibid.*

off England, the *Nautilus* would divert to the Greenland Sea on a scientific mission to explore under the ice. Attainment of the pole had been desirable, but not a critical objective. We had wanted to test the ship and its equipment in this new environment and to train ourselves for further exploration of the Arctic. Thus, on September 1, 1957, the *Nautilus* dived under the pack for the first time. Less than 10 days later the time allotted for this mission had run out, and the *Nautilus* was on her way to her next assignment. She was not as pretty (her bridge area and both periscopes had been damaged by a large block of ice during our first attempt to surface in a polynya) as when we had begun. We had steamed 1,383 miles under ice, had reached 87° N., had lost all gyrocompasses because of a fuse failure, had almost run into the ice-locked coast of northern Greenland, and had successfully surfaced in a polynya. We had not come as close to the pole as we had hoped, but we had learned much that next year would contribute to *Operation Sunshine.*

During the fall and winter of 1957-58, Captain Anderson tackled what he has said was the toughest job he experienced in his naval service: preparing the *Nautilus* for a transpolar voyage in utter secrecy. There were only three other ships' officers, a handful of people in Washington, and one admiral in New London, Connecticut, who knew of the plans. That so many things were done on a top-secret basis is one of the remarkable sidelights of this story. For example, the "ice suit," upward-beaming fathometers, and special sonar equipment were changed; a special high-latitude modification was made on the two gyrocompasses; an inertial-navigation system was installed by North American engineers; cold weather clothing, special publications, and charts were ordered and loaded on board; and a special set of charts was produced by the Hydrographic Office to replace the aircraft navigation charts used in 1957.

After a trip up the west coast, the *Nautilus* departed Seattle, Washington, on June 9, 1958, ostensibly en route to Panama. Instead, Captain Anderson announced to the crew that the destination was Portland, England, via the North Pole.

Our trip was short lived, less than a week. Adverse weather had blocked our path by rafted ice. In the Chukchi Sea, with only 20 feet of water under the keel, an ice ridge cleared the top of the ship by a scant 5 feet. Captain Anderson decided that the *Nautilus* should lay over at Pearl Harbor, Hawaii, until conditions improved.

Conditions did improve, and at 8 P.M., July 22, 1958, the *Nautilus* departed Pearl Harbor. The first leg of the trip was a submerged transit. It went well: a good position check by fathometer as we crossed the well-plotted Aleutian Trench; radar-range and periscope-bearing fixes as we passed between Herbert and Yunaska Islands; a fix and ice-free water on the western side of St. Lawrence Island; and, just before transiting Bering Strait, a visual fix by periscope on Fairway Rock and the Diomede Islands. We had gone 2,901 miles in 6 days, 4 hours, and 9 minutes; an average of 19.6 knots—a record run. No other submarine then operating could duplicate it; relatively few surface vessels had the speed and endurance to better it.

July 30 and 31 were the frustrating days of the trip. Plans were to find 50 fathoms of ice-free water at 73° N. The pack edge, however, was at 72°24′ N. The *Nautilus* probed the pack, surfaced, and submerged. Fog, rain, maverick ice, and large floes all seemed to block our path as we slowly felt our way toward Point Barrow. Just north of Point Franklin, Alaska, radar showed that we had rounded the southern corner of the pack and were aimed toward the Barrow Sea Valley, the deepwater gateway to the western Arctic Basin. As we moved into the valley and increased speed to 18 knots, it was, to quote Captain Anderson, ". . . like pulling onto an expressway from a crowded street." At 8:52 A.M. on August 1, on the 155th meridian, the helmsman was ordered to, " 'Come left to north.' "[3] Dead ahead, 1,094 miles away, lay the North Pole.

Everything went well. As we sped along, our fathometers (pointing up and down) collected during each hour more precise data on the ice and the Arctic Basin floor than had been assembled in all history. We found the unexpected (e.g., near 77° N. the water shoaled suddenly from about 2,100 fathoms to less than 500 fathoms) as well as the expected (e.g., the Lomonosov Ridge at 89° N. [fig. 1].

Four-tenths of a mile from the pole, Captain Anderson stepped up to the mike of the ship's public address system and said:

> All hands—this is the Captain speaking . . . in a few moments *Nautilus* will realize a goal long a dream of mankind—the attainment by ship of the North Geographic Pole. With continued Godspeed, in less than two days we will record an even more significant historic first: the completion of a rapid transpolar voyage from the Pacific to the Atlantic Ocean.

[3] *Ibid.,* p. 209.

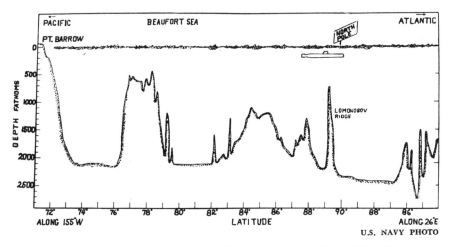

FIGURE 1—The bathymetric profile along the track of the *Nautilus*.

The distance to the Pole is now precisely four-tenths of a mile. As we approach, let us pause in silence dedicated with our thanks for the blessings that have been ours during this remarkable voyage—our prayers for lasting world peace, and in solemn tribute to those who have preceded us, whether in victory or defeat.

Stand by . 10 . . . 8 . . . 6 . . . 4 . . . 3 . . . 2 . . . 1. MARK! August 3, 1958. Time, 2315 (11:15 P.M. Eastern Daylight Saving Time). For the United States and the United States Navy, the North Pole.[4]

A day and a half later we were in open water, 2-foot seas, and brilliant sunlight: the Greenland Sea. On the surface my estimated position, a position by inertial navigation, and a fix from two sunlines (taken about an hour apart) were less than 10 miles apart. *Operation Sunshine* was a success.

[4] *Ibid.*, pp. 222-23.

THE NAVAL ARCTIC RESEARCH LABORATORY AND RESEARCH IN THE ARCTIC BASIN

Max E. Britton

Director, Arctic Program, Earth Sciences Division of the Office of Naval Research since 1966, Dr. Britton was a university professor of botany before and after his service in the U.S. Army during World War II. From 1955 through 1965 he was Scientific Officer for Arctic Research with the Office of Naval Research. Dr. Britton has done field-work in Alaska and other parts of the world.

It is my pleasant task to make a few comments on the Naval Arctic Research Laboratory (NARL) and to place it in some sort of perspective with regard to scientific exploration of the Arctic Basin. I, too, am hampered by the exigencies of program making and inflexible time scales and, in just ten minutes, must cover in some measure that period of scientific exploration and achievement that I believe history will show to be the most intensive and productive to date for the United States in pursuit of knowledge of the Arctic Basin. I have elected to dwell but little on geographical exploration; therefore, perhaps I find myself immediately out of tune with the objectives of this session. But the innumerable aspects of policy, funding, scientific program content, logistic problems, scientific manpower, administrative and services manpower, and so on seemingly without end, are pertinent to exploration. I shall allude to these matters as I go along.

I should point out that the name of the Laboratory was changed to the Naval Arctic Research Laboratory on July 10, 1967, by the

Chief of Naval Research. Before that time it had been the Arctic Research Laboratory. For purposes of simplicity and clarity, I will use NARL throughout this paper.

John Reed has already described the development within the Office of Naval Research (ONR) of the idea of establishing an arctic research laboratory at Point Barrow, and how it became a physical fact in 1947. This marked the start of a land-based program of scientific exploration on the Arctic Slope of Alaska. From the beginning a certain amount of research was conducted at sea; but there had to be much investigation of funding methods, logistic techniques, etc., before significant penetration of the ice pack for scientific purposes could be realized. Through sixteen years of its twenty-one-year history, first as an investigator and since 1955 as an administrator, I have enjoyed a unique opportunity to see NARL grow, to see its problems unfold and sometimes to find solutions for them, to appreciate its strengths and weaknesses, and to develop my own set of emotions and prejudices concerning its entire operation.

Although many of you are quite familiar with NARL, it is perhaps justifiable to give to the uninitiated just a bit of background as to what it is and what it does. First, to me it is a truly remarkable association of university scientists, Government scientists, and administrative and service personnel. In the last analysis a research organization can be no better than its working scientists. NARL has been fortunate from its inception because through it has flowed a steady stream of outstanding, established scientists as well as scores of young graduate students who have gone on to positions of esteem and eminence in arctic research. Hundreds of investigators have made NARL the focal point of their research; many of them have been consistent and faithful customers, returning time and again to pursue their research objectives.

NARL is a rallying point in the Arctic, it is a training ground, and it affords continuity to arctic research. It is expected to furnish a full quota of support to all scientists the Chief of Naval Research sends there; hence, their productivity is very dependent upon the efficiency and skill with which their needs are met. Housing, clothing, food, transportation in the field, laboratory spaces and facilities, field camps and facilities, shop services, advice, guidance—these and innumerable other necessities must be provided. Thus, NARL is in a sense all things to all people once they are in the field. It exists for the support of scientists and does not in itself have a research staff.

Since 1954 the contract for operating NARL has been held by the University of Alaska, which has performed its functions in a truly outstanding manner. The university operates NARL through a director who heads a staff of about seventy administrative and service personnel. Max C. Brewer, the present director, is an exceptionally able and experienced scientist and administrator. He must not only serve the contractual responsibilities of the university, but also perform duties in behalf of the Chief of Naval Research and the representatives of Government agencies who work at NARL or come to the area on Government business.

NARL is a small empire occupying inadequate quarters of a very primitive nature scattered throughout an old construction camp at Point Barrow. Isolation is great, amenities of living are few, and male society predominates. Inadequacies of housing permit only a few families to be in residence. Isolation and abnormal living conditions make personnel difficult to obtain; retention of personnel for more than one or two years is improbable in most cases.

During the past twelve years funds for NARL have increased annually. Although funds are always inadequate, at least this upward trend has been gratifying. During Fiscal Year 1967 more than $1¼ million went into the NARL operation exclusive of the research contracts per se. In the course of a single year several hundred scientists and guests of NARL must be accommodated for varying periods of time. More than a hundred scientists may be in residence at a time working directly at the central laboratories or being supported at more remote sites on land, while others are being cared for on the even more isolated drifting ice stations. The services of NARL are made available to all Government agencies, normally without reimbursement. About one-half the programs at NARL in any year represent Department of the Navy contractor or in-house personnel, and the other half represent other military or civil Federal agencies. By sharing resources and research support in an isolated location, the best interests of the Government are served and much is accomplished that would not otherwise be possible. This experiment in sharing is, in my opinion, one of the most rewarding and enlightened administrative procedures imaginable and is in the broad national interest.

Next I should like to examine briefly the relationship of NARL to research in the Arctic Basin. For my purposes I refer to the basin occupied by the Arctic Ocean—actually an arctic Mediterranean Sea. Located on its shore and in a strategic position, it is not surprising that a naval laboratory engaged in basic research should be interested in the sea. As previously mentioned, several years of experimenting with techniques and methods of funding were necessary before anything but near-shore work could be accomplished.

When I joined ONR in the autumn of 1955, planning for the International Geophysical Year (IGY) was essentially complete. These plans happily included two drifting stations to which John Reed has already referred. I must pass quickly over the success stories of Stations ALPHA and BRAVO that built so well upon the far-sighted efforts of the U.S. Air Force and made such good use of the knowledge gained on ice operations of the late 1940's and early 1950's. I do not wish to pass so quickly, however, as to fail to pay my respect and high regard to the Air Force for its accomplishments and to the personal achievements of such friends as Bert Crary, Louis DeGoes, Joe Fletcher, Jack Streeton, and many others.

During IGY, Louis Quam was wisely planning for an ONR role in future drift station research and, together with Louis DeGoes, he devised a plan under which it was hoped post-IGY operation of BRAVO (on ice island T-3) would be continued by the Air Force, while ONR would assume responsibility for ALPHA. The untimely breakup of ALPHA stifled this plan, but Quam grasped the opportunity of seeking Department of Defense Emergency Fund assistance for the establishment of a new station. Three-quarters of a million dollars from this source plus a similar investment, or more, by the Air Force enabled the establishment and joint operation of Station CHARLIE, which served well for somewhat less than a year, mostly in 1959.

With the demise of CHARLIE, ONR/NARL began experimenting with small, inexpensive pack ice stations. The first of these was ARLIS I, which endured for about nine months in 1960-61. The Air Force continued the support of T-3 until October, 1961. Then followed the remarkable and interesting naval exploit with AR-LIS II, an ice island that was occupied continuously from the spring of 1961 to the spring of 1965, when the station drifted out of the Arctic Basin, transited the Greenland Sea, and was evacuated in Denmark Strait near Iceland. In February, 1962, NARL occupied T-3, which has served significant research programs continuously to the present [fig. 1]. ARLIS III and IV, established on pack ice in 1964 and 1965 respectively, were temporary stations for special purposes during periods of two or three months.

Through their cumulative months of occupancy and thousands of miles of drift over varied tracks, all of these stations have combined to greatly extend our knowledge of the Arctic Ocean. The major research programs, conducted mainly by university groups, have been in the fields of geophysics; physical, chemical, and biological oceanography; geology; meteorology; ice; and underwater acoustics. Such programs are still in progress on T-3 and are planned to continue.

The problem of continuity brings me to an important matter that will constitute my concluding remarks. We have been planning large improvements in our arctic research facilities, including those of drifting stations. A new laboratory and living quarters costing $3 million are under construction at NARL [fig. 2], and authorization for a new aircraft hangar is before Congress this year. Other construction is planned for each year for about the next seven years.

FIGURE 1—The camp buildings, including living quarters and laboratories, on T-3, April 1967.

FIGURE 2—The new NARL building, completed before the volume of conference proceedings went to press.

This is good news! There is also news of a most distressing nature. Very serious budget cuts in ONR have reduced the arctic program nearly $1 million below the 1967 fiscal year level. It is hoped NARL and T-3 can be kept functional, although all programs will be curtailed and many must be terminated. Should similar funding restrictions arise in the 1969 fiscal year, the effects will be too devastating to contemplate. Is this not the time we should seriously explore a merger of forces among all Government agencies with arctic research interests to establish a truly national arctic research laboratory with each agency sharing some portion of the burden? I cannot at this point speak officially for the Navy, but I can and do pledge my personal support to the task.

SESSION II

Highlights of United States Exploration and Research in Antarctica

CHAIRMAN:

James L. Abbot, Jr.

Commander, U.S. Naval Support Force, Antarctica, since February 25, 1967, Rear Admiral Abbot commands all Naval logistic support of U.S. scientific programs in Antarctica. He graduated from the U.S. Naval Academy in 1939.

The two papers of the second session deal with the highlights of the history of U.S. geographical exploration and scientific research in Antarctica. Most of us tend to think of U.S. polar exploration before the International Geophysical Year as being Arctic-oriented, and to a large extent this is true. To the informed historian, however, there is much in the record to indicate that the role of the United States in Antarctica during the nineteenth and twentieth centuries was larger and more important than is generally assumed.

Our role in Antarctica since World War II has become well known; and, since about 1956, a wide variety of carefully planned scientific investigations and an orderly program of exploration have been carried out by the United States each year. As a result, we have acquired a large fund of information about Antarctica. Aspects of some of these recent programs will be commented on by authorities in antarctic mapping and in the biological sciences.

UNITED STATES EXPLORATION AND RESEARCH IN ANTARCTICA THROUGH 1954

Henry M. Dater

Chief of the History and Research Division of the U.S. Naval Support Force, Antarctica, since 1965, Dr. Dater was a university history professor before serving as a Lieutenant Commander in the U.S. Navy during World War II. From 1946 to 1952 he was Chief of the Aviation History and Research Section in the Office of the Chief of Naval Operations; from 1952 to 1956 he was Deputy Historian, Office of the Secretary of Defense; and from 1956 to 1965 he was Historian, U.S. Antarctic Projects Office.

To no one, least of all to me, should be given the task of summarizing 130 years of antarctic history in twenty minutes. After all, I am of the generation that believed Antarctica was a place invented by Rear Admiral Richard E. Byrd with the help of a boy scout named Paul A. Siple. It was only when I became associated with the antarctic program that I began to appreciate the complexity of the subject. Perhaps I should retreat to the simplicity of my original concept, but, alas, this is no longer possible. The innocence of youth is gone, even though the wisdom of age may not be present.

Rather than try to present the chain of events, or even their highlights, in a dreary chronology, I shall attempt to set forth the essence of the U.S. contribution to the investigation of Antarctica. Perhaps, in this approach, some of the highlights will emerge in perspective. To attain my objective is difficult because, to my mind, no history of the Antarctic has yet been written. This statement is not meant to disparage the many authors who have skillfully set forth its annals, but only to point out that the history of Antarctica will not be completely understood until the events themselves are related to ambience and time.[1]

To illustrate the point, the great voyages of Bouvet de Lozier, Yves de Kerguelen-Tremarec, and James Cook were possible only with knowledge of the antiscorbutic properties of citrus fruits. Likewise, the waning of U.S. interest in oceanic exploration after the Civil War is related to the need of developing a trans-Mississippian "empire": the capital that once had been risked in maritime commerce was diverted to land transportation. And consider how much of today's antarctic program grows from the development of aircraft and of equipment capable of probing the upper atmosphere. The Antarctic may be the most isolated area on earth, but it is not divorced from the rest of the globe. Its history is shaped by the same economic, political, social, technological, and scientific tides that mold the rest of the world.

Today, the economic interest of the United States in the Antarctic is minimal, but the first Americans to visit the area, the sealers, came here in search of profit. It is possible that one of them was the first to sight the continent, and certainly, Nathaniel B. Palmer, sailing out of Stonington, Connecticut, did so on November 17, 1820. On February 7, 1821, a colleague from the same state, John Davis of New Haven, made the first known landing on its shore—this in the vicinity of Hughes Bay. No man is devoid of curiosity, and some sealers made sketch maps of the shores and islands that they had visited; others brought back collections of mineral specimens.

Though sealing continued through the remainder of the nineteenth century and constitutes an important but little-known part of our maritime history, the sealer's principal contributions to our knowledge of Antarctica came before 1830. During 1829 and 1830 three sailing vessels carried the first U.S. scientists, including James Eights, of Albany, New York, to the Antarctic. The papers that Eights published after his return contain observations and deductions that remain valid.[2]

---

[1] For general accounts see: Commander, U.S. Naval Support Force, Antarctica, *Introduction to Antarctica* (October, 1957, and later revisions); Laurence P. Kirwan, *A History of Polar Exploration* (New York, 1960); Hugh R. Mill, *The Siege of the South Pole* (London, 1905); and Walter Sullivan, *Quest for a Continent* (New York, 1957).

[2] *Bulletin of the United States Antarctic Projects Officer* (hereafter cited as *Bulletin*), IV (October, 1962), 20; Kenneth J. Bertrand, "American Activity in the Early History of Antarctica," *Bulletin*, VI (December, 1964), 12-14; Edmund Fanning, *Voy-*

Those who had supported Eights and his colleagues had hoped to recapture their investment from profits of sealing. When their venture failed, they turned to the Government for support and joined their efforts with the maritime interests, which wanted the Navy to survey the reefs and unknown islands of the South Pacific where too many U.S. ships were being wrecked and the survivors maltreated by resentful natives. Congress, listening to their pleas, voted the necessary funds and directed the Navy Department to mount the expedition.

Such was the genesis of the United States Exploring Expedition of 1838-42, commonly called the Wilkes Expedition after its commander, Lieutenant Charles Wilkes [fig. 1]. Considering only the antarctic part of his trip, Wilkes' accomplishments were remarkable. In his first season (1839) he visited the tip of the Antarctic Peninsula, and one of his five ships (the *Flying Fish,* a converted harbor-pilot boat of 96 tons) penetrated the ice pack off Thurston Island to 70° S. The second year he sailed from Sydney, Australia. During January and February, 1840, he sighted enough points along approximately 1,500 miles of coast, from 160° E. to 100° E., to establish the existence of the southernmost continent [fig. 2]. Along the way he made many observations and collected numerous specimens of scientific interest.[3]

Unfortunately, the promising beginnings of scientific exploration established by Wilkes were not followed up. On the eve of the Civil War, Commander Matthew Fontaine Maury, head of the Navy's Depot of Charts and Instruments (the ancestor of the present Oceanographic Office), tried unsuccessfully to create interest in an international investigation of the Antarctic.[4] Almost a century elapsed before Maury's suggestion of a multinational effort was taken up in the form of the International Geophysical Year.

ages Around the World, passim (New York, 1833) ; Mill, *op. cit.,* pp. 91-113; Philip I. Mitterling, *America in the Antarctic to 1840* (Urbana, Ill., 1959), pp. 19-100; and Edouard A. Stackpole, *The Voyage of the Huron and the Huntress,* passim (Mystic, Connecticut, 1955).

[3] Bertrand, "Geographical Exploration by the United States," in *The Pacific Basin, A History of Its Geographical Exploration,* Herman R. Friis (ed.), (New York, 1967), pp. 264-268; Bertrand, "Wilkes' Antarctic Discoveries Now Fully Confirmed," *Bulletin,* I (February, 1960), 19-22; Mill, *op. cit.,* pp. 211-248; and Mitterling, *op. cit.,* pp. 101-168.

[4] Friis, "Matthew Fontaine Maury, Captain, U.S. Navy," *Bulletin,* I (February, 1960), 23-29.

FIGURE 1—Charles Wilkes

FIGURE 2—The U.S.S. *Vincennes,* Wilkes' flagship, off the coast of Antarctica, January 1840.

The Wilkes Expedition and the next Government-sponsored expedition to the Antarctic Continent occurred exactly 100 years apart. During this long period, two small scientific expeditions touched the fringes of the antarctic area. Two warships visited the Kerguelen Islands in 1874 to observe the transit of Venus. In 1915-16 the research vessel *Carnegie* circumnavigated the sub-Antarctic, stopping at South Georgia and trying unsuccessfully to land a party on Bouvet Island.[5] Whatever public interest there was in the United States for polar exploration during the late nineteenth and early twentieth centuries was directed northward.

If the researcher scratches around hard enough, he can find a few Americans who joined antarctic expeditions of other nations during this period. Frederick A. Cook served as medical officer on the Adrien de Gerlache expedition of 1897-99.[6] There was an American, disguised as a leading stoker, Royal Navy, on the first Scott expedition; another passed himself off as a Canadian on Shackleton's Imperial Trans-Antarctic Expedition.[7] More independently, Robert C. Murphy and José G. Correia managed to work their way to South Georgia Island where they studied and collected birds in 1912 and 1913.[8]

After World War I, one man—Rear Admiral Richard E. Byrd —revived the interest of the American people in the Antarctic. He did this on his own initiative, using private funds. In the beginning, this was largely due to the enthusiasm for aviation that was so prevalent in the 1920's. By following up his 1928-30 expedition with a second (1933-35), Byrd fixed Antarctica permanently in the American consciousness.[9] An examination of these two expeditions will lead us closer to determining what has been the essence of the U.S. contribution to antarctic exploration.

At the time, the public imagination was most struck by Byrd's

[5] Brian Roberts, *Chronological List of Antarctic Expeditions* (Cambridge, England, 1958), pp. 129 and 197. The book was reprinted from *Polar Record*, IX (May, 1958), 97-134; and *Ibid.* (September, 1958), 191-239.

[6] Frederick A. Cook, *Through the First Antarctic Night, 1898-1899* (New York, 1900).

[7] Edward A. Wilson, *Diary of the 'Discovery' Expedition to the Antarctic Regions, 1901-1904* (London, 1966), p. 286; and *Bulletin*, VI (December, 1964), 12.

[8] Robert C. Murphy, *Oceanic Birds of South America*, I (New York, 1936), 25-26.

[9] The best sources for Richard E. Byrd's expeditions are his own books: *Little America* (New York, 1930); *Discovery* (New York, 1935); and *Alone* (New York, 1938).

flight over the South Pole on November 29, 1929, and by the months in 1934 that he spent at Advance Base on the Ross Ice Shelf, 123 miles south of Little America II. In retrospect, the discoveries in Byrd Land and the scientific work seem more important.

Byrd's enduring fame perhaps rests on his introducing and adapting modern technology to the area more than anything else. A comparison between somewhat parallel experiences of Byrd and Robert F. Scott will suffice to illustrate the importance of Byrd's technological innovations. In March, 1912, Scott, returning from the South Pole, found himself marooned by a blizzard a scant eleven miles from his next depot, debilitated by scurvy, and without means of communicating either with his base or the search parties that might have rescued him. Just seventeen years later, in March, 1929, when Byrd failed to hear by radio from a field party, he flew to its assistance; and when a storm blew up that prevented his return to Little America I, he was able to keep in touch by radio with his base, with dog teams on the trail, and with New Zealand. He even managed to transact business with New York. While in the field, he ate a scientifically blended, if not too appetizing, pemmican that contained not only ample nourishment but also the vitamins necessary to prevent dietary-deficiency diseases, including scurvy.[10]

It is always a temptation to overstate Byrd's role as an innovator. For example, Sir Hubert Wilkins preceded him by a few months in introducing to the Antarctic the airplane equipped for photographic reconnaissance.[11] While Byrd's 1933-35 expedition was the first to use tracked vehicles with success, Scott had tried them on his second expedition, 1910-13.[12] One of Byrd's many strengths, however, was that he carefully studied the equipment and techniques of his predecessors, modifying them as need be and integrating them with newer developments. His scientific programs for the most part followed lines already well established. On his second expedition, however, he extended cosmic-ray research to the Antarctic, and, by adapting

[10] Byrd, *Little America*, pp. 159-187.

[11] John Grierson, *Challenge to the Poles* (Hamden, Connecticut, 1964), pp. 181-185; W. L. G. Joerg, *Brief History of Polar Exploration Since the Introduction of Flying* (New York, 1930), pp. 3-10; and Hubert Wilkins, "The Wilkins-Hearst Antarctic Expedition, 1928-1929," *The Geographical Review*, XIX (July, 1929), 353-376.

[12] Leonard Huxley (comp.), *Scott's Last Expedition*, I (New York, 1913), 301-312. Even though his vehicles broke down quickly, Scott believed in them as the future form of transportation in the Antarctic; see *Ibid.* pp. 278-279.

the seismic techniques of petroleum exploration to glaciology, he opened the way to determination of ice thickness.[13]

Finally, it has been said of Byrd that not the least of his talents was the ability to obtain the funds he needed from men of great wealth. The more one studies his first two expeditions, the less surprising this seems. Like many of his backers, Byrd possessed managerial talents of a very high order. Before setting forth, he planned thoroughly and selected both personnel and equipment with care. In operation, he showed great flexibility, being unafraid to modify existing plans or to improvise if necessary. Finally, he was cautious without being timid. The entrepreneurs to whom he applied for support must have found in him one of themselves—except that where they sought profits, he looked for fame and glory and the advancement of human knowledge.[14]

Another motive for antarctic exploration, besides the desire for gain and the search for scientific truth, was nationalism. Byrd was patriotic, as was his contemporary, Lincoln Ellsworth, whose transantarctic flight in 1935 was certainly one of the most courageous events in antarctic annals.[15] Both men at times laid claim to territory in the name of the United States. Nationalism was not confined to individual expression. Political goals played an important part in the creation of the United States Antarctic Service (USAS) in 1939, as they were to do after World War II in *Operation Highjump*.

The fact that only one expedition was held under the USAS has obscured its significance. Too often it has been treated as a third Byrd expedition, which in part it was, but only in part. The USAS was created to operate permanent stations and, by doing so, to strengthen the position of the United States in regard to its territorial claims. Because permanent occupancy was planned, the Government turned to the National Research Council of the National Academy of Sciences to develop a comprehensive scientific program. By making Byrd head of the USAS, it was assured that the application of his managerial techniques would be transferred from private to public enterprise.

[13] G. de Q. Robin (ed.), "Glaciology," *Annals of the International Geophysical Year*, XLI (New York, 1967), 36; and Sullivan, *op. cit.*, pp. 97-98.

[14] No adequate biography of Byrd exists. His preoccupation with planning and organization, however, runs through both *Little America* and *Discovery*.

[15] Lincoln Ellsworth, *Beyond Horizons* (New York, 1937), pp. 316-345.

FIGURE 3—The U.S.M.S. *North Star* and the U.S.S. *Bear* at Little America III during the United States Antarctic Service Expedition.

The single expedition (1939-41) was a success [fig. 3]. Two bases were occupied: one at Little America III (West Base) under Paul A. Siple; the other on Stonington Island (East Base) off the west coast of the Antarctic Peninsula, under Richard B. Black. Exploratory flights and long overland journeys were made. It is probable that more scientific work was done than on any previous expedition, but too little of it ever saw light. When the time came to replace the personnel and to resupply the bases, the war in Europe threatened to spread to the United States. Consequently, the bases were closed, the members of the expedition returned to the United States, and most of them were absorbed by war service before they could write up the results of their research.[16]

---

[16] The U.S. Antarctic Service Expedition is the most poorly reported major expedition in antarctic history. The best account of it is in Sullivan, *op. cit.*, pp. 137-170. For the scientific work of the expedition see: *Reports on Scientific Results of the United*

Towaid the end of World War II, or shortly thereafter, Argentina, Britain, and Chile took up the idea of permanent bases. The United States did not. Instead, the Navy developed what it called Antarctic Development Projects. The concept behind these projects was never clearly formulated, but the main elements were a desire to test equipment under polar conditions in an area where the United States could not be accused of provocation; the reinforcement of this country's territorial position by a recurrent presence, if not by occupancy; and scientific investigation.[17]

The first Antarctic Developments Project took place during the austral summer of 1946-47 and was called *Operation Highjump*. Even today, *Highjump* remains the largest expedition ever sent to the Antarctic. Assigned to it were 13 ships; 33 aircraft; numerous vehicles, tracked and otherwise; and about 4,800 personnel. It has been said that if antarctic experts had been consulted, some items that the Navy furnished the expedition would not have been sent. Such criticism misses the point. The Navy wanted to test existing equipment and procedures for their adaptability to polar operations, and it had no choice but to start with what was on hand from World War II. It is amazing how much of what *Highjump* took to Antarctica proved useful for polar exploration and investigation. For the first time there appeared those three mainstays of today's operations: icebreakers, helicopters, and aircraft with combination ski-wheel landing gear. Furthermore, the aircraft were equipped with radar (indispensable for navigation) and trimetrogon camera installations, which are the heart of aerial photomapping. Several types of tracked vehicles, almost all originally designed for amphibious operations in tropical waters, were tried out. Many of them worked surprisingly well, and Weasels can still be found working stoutly at the bases of half a dozen nations [fig. 4].

The short time the expedition spent in the Antarctic—about two months—precluded meaningful scientific work in some fields. However, with three scattered task groups taking simultaneous

---

States Antarctic Service Expedition, 1939-1941, Vol. 89 of Proceedings of the American Philosophical Society (Philadelphia, April, 1945); and National Archives, *Records of the United States Antarctic Service,* Preliminary Inventory No. 90 (Washington, 1955).

[17] Chief of Naval Operations to the Commanders-in-Chief of the Atlantic and Pacific Fleets, August 26, 1946, included as Enclosure A in Commander, Task Force 68, *Report on Antarctic Developments Project, 1947 (Operation Highjump)* [1947], CTF68/A9/rkd, Serial 0184.

FIGURE 4—A Weasel in the field, 1967.

weather observations, new light was shed on the movements of air masses and frontal systems. Over 70,000 aerial photographs were taken on 64 flights. Significant flights were made inland by aircraft operating from Little America IV. Task groups composed of seaplane tenders and flying boats stationed east and west of Ross Sea fanned out to survey the continent's coastline. In all, 60 percent of it was seen, 25 percent for the first time. Of the part seen, about 40 percent was discovered to have been incorrectly plotted in the past. Finally, there was the intangible of personal experience. Many individuals who participated in *Highjump* contributed, a decade later, to *Operation Deep Freeze* and the International Geophysical Year.[18]

The most important achievement of *Highjump*, its aerial photography, was flawed because too few ground-control points had been established to permit map construction. The second Antarctic Developments Project, 1947-48 (*Operation Windmill*), had as its principal objective the correction of this deficiency. The two icebreakers assigned to the project were equipped with helicopters to carry ashore topographic engineers [fig. 5]. They would determine the geographical coordinates of selected features for use as reference points in turning *Highjump* photography into maps.[19]

[18] *Ibid.;* Bertrand, "A Look at *Operation Highjump* Twenty Years Later," *Antarctic Journal of the United States,* II (January-February, 1967), 5-12; and Sullivan, *op. cit.,* pp. 173-248.
[19] Commander, Task Force 39, *Report of Operations, Second Antarctic Development[s] Project, 1947-1948* [1948], CTF39/A9/rdk, Series 045; Lewis O. Smith, " 'Operation Windmill,' the Second Antarctic Developments Project," *Antarctic Journal of the United States,* III (March-April, 1968), 23-36; and Sullivan, *op. cit.,* pp. 249-261.

FIGURE 5—A HO3S-1 helicopter and the U.S.S. *Burton Island* off Knox Coast in January 1948 during *Operation Windmill*.

FIGURE 6—The U.S.S. *Burton Island* prepares to tow the *Port of Beaumont* out of Marguerite Bay, 1948.

On their way back from Antarctica, the two icebreakers went to the assistance of an expedition occupying the old USAS base on Stonington Island [fig. 6]. Its leader, Finn Ronne, although aided by the loan of large quantities of Government equipment, had succeeded with minimal outlays of cash in what was the last privately conducted expedition by a U.S. citizen or, for that matter, by a private individual of any nation. Considering the resources at his disposal, Ronne's accomplishments were remarkable. An interesting aspect of this expedition was the winter-long presence of two women, the wives of members. (Whether this will form part of the U.S. contribution to antarctic exploration, only time can tell.) More significant, at least for the moment, was the cooperation of Ronne with the British. When Ronne arrived at Stonington Island he found that the British had established a base only a few hundred yards distant on the same island. At first the two parties looked upon one another with some suspicion, but good sense eventually prevailed, and the two cooperated. Together, they achieved more than they possibly could have if they had operated separately.[20]

There was not another U.S. expedition to the Antarctic until those operations which are essentially a part of the International Geophysical Year (IGY). A third Antarctic Developments Project was planned, however, and actually given the name *Highjump II* before it was canceled for budgetary reasons.[21] As far as operations in the field are concerned, one might appropriate T. S. Eliot's phrase and say that the chronology of U.S. activities before 1954 "ends not with a bang but a whimper."

The withdrawal of financial support did not mean that interest in the Antarctic had ceased. Even while the abortive *Highjump II* was being planned, the National Academy of Sciences presented to the State Department a report that was prophetic in its tone. In addition to recommending research in specific scientific fields—which recommendations later formed the basis of the U.S. program during IGY—the document advocated a continuing effort over many years, indicated that the Department of Defense alone had the equipment and experience to provide logistic support, and stated that a scientific

[20] Finn Ronne, *Antarctic Conquest* (New York, 1949). For a British view see Sir Raymond Priestly, "The Background," in Sir Raymond Priestly, Raymond J. Adie, and G. de Q. Robin (eds.), *Antarctic Research* (London, 1964), p. 11.

[21] George J. Dufek, *Operation Deepfreeze* (New York, 1957), pp. 31-32.

program covering the entire antarctic area would have to be international in character.[22]

Antarctica was too important to be long neglected. When in 1953 and 1954 the United States prepared to resume antarctic operations in support of IGY programs, it had 130 years of experience behind it. Many of the lessons derived from this experience were the common property of all nations that had been active in the area. All agreed on the advantages to be gained from international cooperation and on the need in many fields for several years of continuous observation. What made the United States different from others was the depth of its technical know-how and managerial expertise. The essence of the U.S. contribution to antarctic exploration and research was the adaptation of the technology and procedures of its highly industrialized society to the very different environment of Antarctica. In other words, it was the application to a specialized problem of some very typical U.S. talents.

[22] National Academy of Sciences, *Antarctic Research, Elements of a Coordinated Program* (Washington, 1949), reprinted in 1954 for the use of the U.S. National Committee for IGY.

UNITED STATES EXPLORATION AND RESEARCH IN ANTARCTICA FROM 1955

Albert P. Crary

Deputy Director, Division of Environmental Sciences, National Science Foundation, since July 1, 1967, Dr. Crary is at home in the Arctic as well as the Antarctic, having been among the pioneers in the use of ice islands as scientific floating stations in the Arctic Ocean. He was project scientist at the Woods Hole Oceanographic Institute, 1941-42; project scientist at the U.S. Air Force Cambridge Research Center, 1946-60; and Chief Scientist for the Office of Antarctic Programs, National Science Foundation, 1960-66. He served as Deputy Chief Scientist for Antarctica, U.S. National Committee on the International Geophysical Year.

I am delighted to have the privilege of addressing this assembly gathered for the opening of the Center for Polar Archives. This is a great step forward in assuring our country that its polar records will have a proper home and will be available for all time to the students of polar activities. It is a difficult task to assign historical values to contemporary events, but this appears to be my task this morning. What have been the highlights of U.S. exploration and research in Antarctica during the last decade? I am sure that people may not agree on the list of highlights that I am going to give, and I am equally aware that fifty or a hundred years from now opinions may be entirely different.

Archivists must deal with people, and to select the outstanding achievements at any time and place is to pick the people who have been outstanding. Although at the polar regions achievements must result from teamwork, I must nevertheless pay respect to the men who, heroic in the traditional sense or not, have to a large degree guided U.S. efforts in Antarctica since 1955: Rear Admirals Richard E. Byrd, George J. Dufek, David M. Tyree, James R. Reedy, and Fred E. Bakutis; and civilians Alan T. Waterman, Detlev Bronk, Laurence M. Gould, Harry Wexler, and Thomas O. Jones.

The highlights of U.S. exploration in the Antarctic since 1955 have been closely linked with the aircraft. If the eight major achievements I am about to describe were to be narrowed down to a single one, it would be simply the aerial conquest of the continent. Before 1955 many man-months at sea and many man-winters on the continent were necessary for a few man-weeks of work. This no longer is the case. Except for the minority who winter over to keep continuity of observatory data, Antarcticans, more than any other people, are airborne. Because of the aircraft and those who have brought air operations to their present status, it can now be said that the continent has been explored.

It has been my privilege at the National Science Foundation to have been associated with antarctic scientists for the last decade. Scientists in general, inquisitive though they may be, are concerned primarily with their written results, and these are permanently recorded in the scientific journals. Significant scientific highlights will come when the scientists have finished answering the question, "What," and begin answering the question, "Why." The next decade, I predict, will be mainly one of scientific highlights. The stage has been set.

All stories must have a beginning, and the first highlight I want to mention is the voyage of the U.S.S. *Atka,* AGB-3, an American-built icebreaker that had been transferred to the Soviet Navy under the lend-lease program during the last months of World War II. It was returned to the United States after five years of Russian service in the Arctic. Commanded by Captain Glen Jacobsen, the *Atka,* in the austral summer of 1954-55, prepared for U.S. participation in the International Geophysical Year (IGY) by a lonely voyage of some 30,000 miles inspecting possible station sites and surveying the ice front along the Pacific and Atlantic coasts of Antarctica.

The second highlight is the December 20, 1955, flight of the first aircraft in history to land in Antarctica from outside land areas. Eight aircraft were scheduled to make the flight—two P2V Neptunes on skis and two R5D Skymasters on wheels from Christchurch, New Zealand, and two R4D Skytrains and two UF Albatross triphibians from Dunedin, New Zealand. The added proximity of Dunedin to the Antarctic, however, could not make up for the strong headwinds encountered, and the Skytrains and Albatrosses were forced to return. The other four went on to complete the 2,230-mile trip. Admiral Dufek, the first Commander of the U.S. Naval Support Force, Antarctica, had lined up four surface ships between New Zealand and the edge of the sea ice to give these flights weather information, communications, and confidence. The airstrip at McMurdo Sound, prepared by an advance group under Captain Gerald Ketchum, was declared ready on December 19, and on December 20 the planes took off. The pilots were Captain William M. Hawkes; Lieutenant Commanders John H. Torbert, Joseph W. Entrikin, and Henry P. Jorda; and Lieutenant Colonel H. R. Kolp. Hawkes and Torbert, veterans of the earlier *Operation Highjump,* said that the flight was routine.

The next month these four planes and this group of pilots wrote exploration history by the third highlight—the exploratory flights of 1955-56. Figure 1 shows the routes of these round-trip flights: to the geographic pole, to the geomagnetic pole, to the magnetic pole, to "poles of inaccessibility," to the Knox Coast, and to the Weddell Sea. This last flight under Hawkes and Torbert lasted 19 hours and, for exploratory information, was perhaps the most important. It was during this flight that the Pensacola Mountains were discovered, a truly magnificent range stretching over 300 miles in length and forming a bulwark against the East Antarctic ice sheet.

The fourth highlight occurred the following Antarctic summer after the R4D Skytrains had finally flown in from New Zealand with the help of additional fuel tanks. Lieutenant Commander Conrad Shinn and Captain Hawkes, pilots, with Admiral Dufek and Captain Douglas Cordiner aboard as observers, landed the Skytrain *Que Sera Sera* at the geographic South Pole on October 31, 1956. This was the first surface contact with the pole since Captain Robert F. Scott departed 44 years earlier on his tragic overland journey. The surface temperature registered −58° F., and all 15 jet takeoff bottles were needed to unfreeze the skis for takeoff, but the U.S. inland station at the pole was assured.

For the fifth highlight on my list, we return to the surface. Byrd

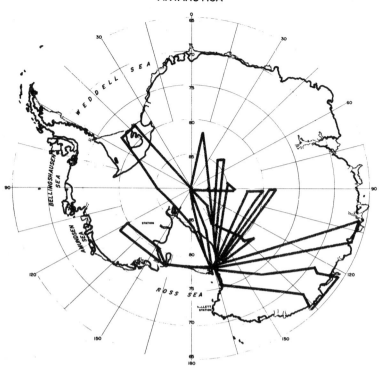

FIGURE 1—The routes of the 1955-56 exploratory flights.

Station was to be installed at 80° S., 120° W., in West Antarctica, 700 miles from the pole toward the Pacific Ocean, by the beginning of IGY on July 1, 1957. The station was to be supported entirely by tractor trail across the crevasse fields from Little America V. The blazing of this trail was a heroic feat that required the two austral summers of 1955-56 and 1956-57 and involved principally the valiant Seabees with their giant 20-ton tractors. The final operation was under Commander Paul Frazier. Assisting him were a few Army men under Major Merle R. Dawson, who had served in Greenland and were specialists in traveling over snow and ice. For the next two seasons the giant tractors thundered across the ice to supply Byrd Station, but they finally gave way to the increasingly efficient air support. This was the last of the U.S. giant surface swings.

These five highlights set the stage for a more detailed examination of the continent. The sixth highlight, an extensive oversnow traverse program, started in 1957 and will be completed in 1969. Civilian scientists with oversnow vehicles have traveled nearly 20,000 miles over inland areas of Antarctica obtaining elevations, ice thicknesses, and annual snow accumulations; learning more about gravity and magnetic fields; and locating nunataks and ice-free mountains.

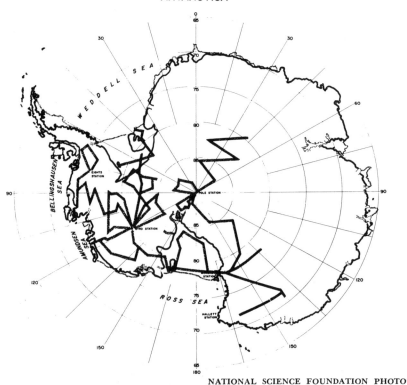

FIGURE 2—The routes, 1957-66, of the U.S. oversnow traverses.

Charles R. Bentley of the University of Wisconsin has had a leading role in these traverses, having been with the first such journey from Little America V to Byrd Station in early 1957 and leading four subsequent summer traverses. Figure 2 shows the extent of the U.S. traverses. These, along with the travels by other nations in the interior and the aerial exploration by the United States and other countries, indicate the thoroughness with which Antarctica has been explored in the last decade.

The early flights over the South Pole and the landing at the pole in 1956 had confirmed the impressions of Roald Amundsen and Scott that this was an endless land of monotonous cold. The seventh highlight is the first winter occupation of the Amundsen-Scott South Pole Station during 1957. Although the pole has been continually occupied since November, 1956, never again will the disappearance of the sun in March bring so much apprehension. True to form, however, it was not survival that worried this courageous group as they passed into the −100° F. temperature, but whether or not their vast array of instruments would be operating at the beginning of IGY. Led by the veteran antarctic scientist, Paul A. Siple, and the young, energetic Lieutenant John Tuck, Jr., their twelve-month stay on the geographic axis was a triumphant climax to all the previous years of antarctic exploration.

The list of accomplishments in Antarctica does not stop here. Every year brings new improvements in methods of operations, in the facilities of the permanent stations, and in the sophistication of recording equipment. The introduction of the long-range C-130 Hercules aircraft, the largest U.S. plane outfitted with skis, permits landing in any part of Antarctica. Station modular units that fit into the C-130 planes make it possible to install inland stations with a minimum of effort. The use of the UH-1B turbine helicopter permits geologists and surveyors to land on high mountain peaks. Electronic distance-measuring devices make it easy to lay out survey base lines and to obtain information about ice movements. Electromagnetic ice sounding and satellite navigation, photography, and readout are currently in the forefront of technical triumph in Antarctica.

However, for my eighth highlight in the last decade in the Antarctic, I have chosen one that I feel meets all criteria for outstanding exploratory accomplishment—the Antarctic Treaty. Although it was the work of twelve nations that brought the unique treaty to fruition, and not solely that of the United States, it was here in our Capitol in December, 1959, that the treaty was signed. Historically, the consequences of the treaty may far outstrip the other events that I have mentioned. It is a fitting reward for the efforts of many people from many lands that this vast and silent continent should belong to all mankind.

UNITED STATES GEOLOGICAL SURVEY ANTARCTIC MAPPING OPERATIONS

Rupert B. Southard, Jr.

Assistant Chief Topographic Engineer for Plans and Program Development, U.S. Geological Survey, Mr. Southard has been closely associated with the U.S. antarctic mapping program since 1961. He has been with the U.S. Geological Survey since the end of World War II except for service with the Marine Corps during the Korean War.

It is my pleasure to have the opportunity to talk to you this morning on the mapping program of Antarctica. Although my remarks are concerned with highlights of the United States Geological Survey (USGS) antarctic mapping operations, I want to point out at the start that we at the Survey do not presume to take full credit for the success of the mapping program. Perhaps more than any other single discipline in the Antarctic, mapping requires the close support of the U.S. Naval Support Force, Antarctica (Task Force 43), especially Naval Air Development Squadron Six (VX-6).[1] Without their photographs our program would be impossible. Mapping priorities are the result of consultations with the National Science Foundation (NSF), which funds our mapping as part of the U.S. Antarctic Research Program (USARP). We do take credit for producing the maps, but the overall mapping program is a highly integrated effort.

Simply stated, it is the responsibility of the Survey to produce maps at whatever scales are required to support USARP activities. Systematic photogrammetric mapping requires three distinct and separate operations: procurement of aerial photography, establish-

[1] VX-6 is attached to TF-43 while in Antarctica and is responsible for all air logistics and procurement of aerial photography.

ment of ground control, and compilation of the map. Each of these operations requires considerable advance planning and usually is time consuming. Maps are not turned out overnight, which perhaps is the reason that fewer than half of the nations participating in the International Geophysical Year (IGY) program in Antarctica conducted topographic mapping activities during 1957 and 1958. In any event, it was not until it became apparent that antarctic investigations were going to continue long after IGY that the mapping of Antarctica was begun in earnest as part of a long-range program of scientific research. A look at the status of our mapping in 1962—halfway through the recently completed decade of international cooperation in Antarctica—would show considerable activity but few published maps. Only 11 maps, all at 1:500,000 scale and all of East Antarctica, had been published, and they were all started before IGY, using photographs and control points obtained during *Operations Highjump* and *Windmill.*

The first objective of the USARP mapping program is to produce 1:250,000-scale maps with 200-meter contours of all of the mountainous and coastal areas of West Antarctica. An important by-product of this mapping is the unpublished series of 1:50,000-scale planimetric manuscripts of mountainous areas, which many USARP scientists prefer to use to record the results of their early field investigations. The NSF-USGS Plan for Optical Aerial Mapping Photography reflects the foreseeable map requirements of USARP scientists [fig. 1] and is revised periodically to take into account our increasing knowledge of the areas to be mapped and the seasonal accomplishments of the photography program. The current plan calls for mapping from 158° E. clockwise to 8° W., exclusive of the Antarctic Peninsula north of 68° S. The previous version of the plan called for mapping 1,118,000 square miles in 264 sheets at 1:250,000 scale. Information developed from recent photoreconnaissance flights showed that 65 of these sheets would be basically featureless with 1:250,000-scale mapping, and they were eliminated from the plan. In addition, the mapping accomplishments of Norway, Belgium, and South Africa along the Princess Astrid Coast eliminated the requirement for 30 sheets. Accordingly, the current plan is to map 169 sheets at 1:250,000 scale covering 720,800 square miles, a reduction of 94 sheets and 397,200 square miles from the previous plan.

The tricamera system used in Antarctica was developed for re-

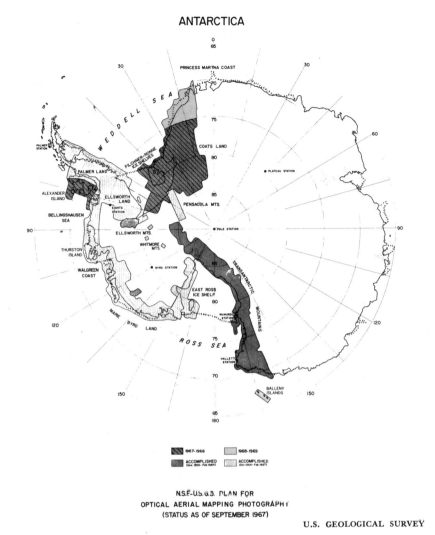

N.S.F.-U.S.G.S. PLAN FOR
OPTICAL AERIAL MAPPING PHOTOGRAPHY
(STATUS AS OF SEPTEMBER 1967)

U.S. GEOLOGICAL SURVEY

FIGURE 1—The status of NSF-USGS plans for aerial mapping photography in Antarctica, September 1967.

connaissance mapping and is still considered the best available method for obtaining photography for antarctic mapping. Three cameras are mounted in the aircraft so that the center camera takes a vertical photograph at the same time that the other two, depressed 30° from the horizon, take photographs to the left and right of the flight path. Tricamera antarctic photography taken by the United States totals 1,628,615 square miles.

Before the 1960-61 season, photographic coverage totaled 689,-000 square miles, but this consisted mostly of exploratory reconnaissance and marginal coverage, which was considered inadequate for the 1:250,000-scale mapping program. Accordingly, NSF requested

the Survey to prepare detailed specifications for aerial mapping photography, and we have performed this task for eight years. To expe-
dite inspection and acceptance of photography for USARP, we have
stationed a Survey photogrammetric specialist in New Zealand and
Antarctica every season since 1960 to inspect all film as the missions
are flown. He recommends reflights and, when feasible, acts as in-
flight adviser and visual navigator during photographic mapping
flights. Mapping-quality photography obtained by VX-6 since 1960
totals 939,615 square miles—an outstanding accomplishment. Seasonal totals are far from constant: 118,800 square miles during *Deep
Freeze 61;* 105,000 during *Deep Freeze 62;* 44,000 during *Deep
Freeze 63;* 14,700 during *Deep Freeze 64,* when the LP-2J (P2V)
Neptunes were phased out and the C-121J Super Constellation was
the mapping aircraft; 182,115 during *Deep Freeze 65,* reflecting primarily the photoconfiguration of one of the LC-130F Hercules; 135,-
000 during *Deep Freeze 66;* and 340,000 during *Deep Freeze 67.*
Plans for the coming season total 401,000 square miles of photography—a tall order for VX-6, but one that we know they will do their
best to accomplish.

The Survey has sent engineers to Antarctica every year for ten
years to establish mapping control. For the first few years our men
were assigned to oversnow geophysical traverses as navigators, and
mapping control was established on an opportunity basis. The features to be mapped were seldom visited, and accurate identification
of intersected points was difficult, since aerial photographs were not
available to field parties. Positions were based on solar observations,
and the work was not of a high order of accuracy. The first significant
step toward improving this situation occurred during the 1961-62
field season: Army gas-turbine helicopters were made available for
the exclusive use of a Geological Survey topographic mapping party.
For the first time control engineers could move quickly to take advantage of short periods of good weather, and the high performance
characteristics of the UH-1B helicopters enabled the party to land on
mountain peaks with pressure altitudes up to 13,500 feet above sea
level. Photographs of the area were available for detailed planning of
the operation. Electronic distance-measuring instruments were used
for quick, accurate measurement of distances between primary control points, and photoidentifiable features were intersected up to 50
miles on either side of the main traverse. The results of the first two

seasons during which this method was used are impressive: *Projects Topo North, South, East,* and *West* established control for the mapping of 180,000 square miles along the Transantarctic Mountains while traversing over 3,155 miles. This is equal to a traverse from Mexico City to Juneau, Alaska, with control in a strip 56 miles wide along this line. Similar methods have been used by our engineers since 1963 to control other areas in Antarctica. Inasmuch as the helicopters are now used to support several disciplines, the results have not been as productive from a purely mapping viewpoint. As a coordinated USARP effort, however, these multidisciplinary traverses must be considered to be one of the highlights of modern antarctic exploration, and the Survey is proud to have been able to pioneer the use of this technique in Antarctica.

The combined efforts of all those involved in the mapping program have enabled the Survey to compile and publish 34 sheets covering 135,000 square miles, 20 percent of the revised 1:250,000-scale program. In compilation are 48 sheets covering 239,200 square miles, approximately 28 percent of the program, which should be published between now and 1971 if our current production rate continues unchanged. Aerial photography has been obtained for 54 additional sheets along the Walgreen and Eights Coasts, 32 percent of the programmed mapping. Ground control for 22 of these 54 sheets is scheduled for completion as part of this year's Byrd Land Survey, and the remaining 32 of these sheets will be controlled between 1969 and 1972. The area included in 33 sheets, the remaining 20 percent of the program, is scheduled for aerial photography during the next two austral summers. If this year's aerial photographic program is 100 percent successful, photographs for 26 of these sheets will be completed, leaving only 7 sheets to be photographed the following year.

A recent addition to our mapping program is the interim 1:500,000-scale, shaded-relief sketch map series. Every scientist needs to have a map of the area in which his investigation is to be conducted when he goes to the field for the first time. The sketch map series is designed to satisfy this need by utilizing available aerial photographs and existing (often sparse) ground control to map areas before initial penetration by USARP parties. At present (1967) approximately 150,000 square miles are mapped in this series, and 262,000 square miles are in compilation. Most of the areas covered by the sketch map series will be mapped later as part of the standard 1:250,000-scale topographic mapping program.

During the second meeting of the Scientific Committee on Antarctic Research (SCAR) in Moscow, 1958, a temporary Working Group on Cartography was authorized. At a later SCAR meeting it was converted to a permanent Working Group on Geodesy and Cartography. As a result of the activities of the Working Group, SCAR has made a series of formal recommendations to member governments pertaining to standards, technical specifications, and symbols for antarctic surveys and maps. Geological Survey maps of Antarctica conform to these recommendations. Another SCAR recommendation called for the exchange between member nations of all cartographic data of areas within the interest of SCAR. The Working Group maintains and regularly distributes a current list of topographic maps and aeronautical and hydrographic charts of the Antarctic. The focal point within the United States for the international exchange of this data is the Geological Survey, in its function as the U.S. Antarctic Mapping Center. It also maintains the Antarctic Map and Aerial Photography Library in Silver Spring, Maryland, in which are stored some 1,200 foreign and United States maps and charts of Antarctica and nearly 250,000 aerial photographs, including most of those taken during *Operation Highjump* and Finn Ronne's expedition, and all of those taken during *Deep Freeze*. Orders for any of this material can be placed with the library, and USARP scientists are encouraged to inspect available data before leaving for Antarctica.

There is a continuing national effort to improve the techniques and facilities being used in the topographic mapping of Antarctica. For example, two advisory groups review current practices and investigate others for possible use. These are the Technical Advisory Committee on Antarctic Mapping and the Panel on Geodesy and Cartography of the Committee on Polar Research, National Academy of Sciences. Under scrutiny are those developments in satellite geodesy and cartography that show promise of being applicable to the Antarctic. Plans for geodetic ties from Antarctica to other continents are well advanced, and though this program will not involve Geological Survey personnel, we look forward to the day when our antarctic surveys can be placed on a worldwide geodetic datum. The value of space photography for antarctic mapping has already been demonstrated by the Survey. Photographs from the Nimbus weather satellite have been used to reposition Mount Siple approximately 45 miles west of its previously recorded position and to delineate other features in West Antarctica. The Space Technology Applications Office of the Survey conducts a continuing research program designed to apply space-obtained data to cartographic mapping, and research has suggested that small- and medium-scale maps can be constructed from satellite photography. It is hoped that the Survey will have an opportunity to use these techniques before the task of mapping Antarctica is completed—if not for the 1:250,000 program, then perhaps for the 1:1,000,000-scale series that has been recommended to cover those areas of Antarctica not worthy of mapping at 1:250,000.

My remarks today have only touched on the most important aspects of the antarctic topographic mapping program. I hope they have been sufficient to give you an understanding of why we at the Geological Survey are proud of our efforts and are pleased to be a part of the international scientific effort in Antarctica.

THE LOGISTIC AND TECHNOLOGICAL CONTRIBUTION OF THE UNITED STATES TO ANTARCTIC BIOLOGICAL RESEARCH

William J. L. Sladen

Dr. Sladen was born in England and educated at the University of London and Oxford University. He was an officer and biologist on the Falkland Islands Dependencies Survey, British Antarctic Expedition, 1947-51. Since that time he has continued to do extensive fieldwork and research in the Arctic and Antarctic. Dr. Sladen is a professor of medicine and biology in the School of Hygiene and Public Health, The Johns Hopkins University.

Antarctic research offers scientists rare opportunities in these days of extreme specialization for multidisciplinary experiences and co-operation. I am repeatedly impressed by this when I attend the National Science Foundation U.S. Antarctic Research Program (USARP) pre-antarctic orientation program at Skyland, Virginia. Scientists from all walks of life, the meteorologists, geologists, seismologists, and biologists gather together, outline their programs, and inform other scientists of their ambitions, aims, and research objectives for the coming antarctic season. Later, when living together in a small isolated antarctic community (I am thinking particularly of those who winter over), scientists are as much exposed to the disciplines of their colleagues as to their beards and personal idiosyncrasies. This multidisciplinary approach in a highly specialized age is a very attractive feature of antarctic research, and there is every reason to believe it will continue this way.

My comments will be chiefly concerned with the biological and medical sciences, since these are my particular interests. Before and during the International Geophysical Year (IGY), very little attention was paid to these disciplines in U.S. antarctic research. Since 1957 there has been an enormous amount of work done that is beginning to get published in the many biological journals. Presently USARP's biological program has some twenty-five projects in eighteen universities in the disciplines of botany, biochemistry, mammalogy, ornithology, microbiology, invertebrate ecology, marine biology, and physiology (to mention a few). About a hundred professional biologists and their assistants are involved in fieldwork, to say nothing of the increasing number of people working up scientific results of this fieldwork.

U.S. logistic support has proved an invaluable aid to antarctic research. There is no better way to illustrate this than by quoting from Apsley Cherry-Garrard's diary printed in the second volume of *Scott's Last Expedition,* regarding the winter journey he made to Cape Crozier, Ross Island, with Edward Wilson (referred to as Bill) and Henry Bowers (referred to as Birdie) from late June to early August, 1911. This was written after their return from a visit to the Emperor Penguin, *Aptenodytes forsteri,* rookery at Cape Crozier.

> It is also difficult already, after two nights' rest, with a dozen men all round anticipating your every wish, and with the new comfortable life of the hut all round you, to realise [sic] completely how bad the last few weeks have been, how at times one hardly cared whether we got through or not, so long as (I speak for myself) if I was to go under it would not take very long. Although our weights are not very different, I am only 1½ lb. and Bill and Birdie 3½ lbs. lighter than when we started. We were very done when we got in, falling asleep on the march, and unable to get into our finnesko or eat our meals without falling asleep. Although we were doing good marches up to the end, we were pulling slow and weak, and the cold was getting at us in a way in which it had never touched us before. Our fingers were positive agony immediately we took them out of our mits, and to undo a lashing took a very long time. The night we got in Scott said he thought it was the hardest journey which had ever been made. Bill says it was infinitely worse than the Southern Journey in 1902-3. I would like to put it on record that Captain

Scott considered this journey to be the hardest which had ever
been done. This was a well-considered judgment.[1]

The objective of Wilson's party was to collect the early embryos of the Emperor Penguin.[2] Because this penguin lays and in-
cubates its egg on sea ice between May and August, these British
explorers made this now famous journey by foot in winter darkness.
It took them 36 days from Hut Point, McMurdo, and back. At times
they had to contend with 100 m.p.h. winds and temperatures as low
as −70° F (−56.7° C).

Visiting this same Emperor Penguin rookery in the austral
spring of 1965, our Johns Hopkins University group was transported
there by U.S. Navy helicopter from McMurdo. "The Worst Journey
in the World," as described by Cherry-Garrard, which had taken
them 18 days from Hut Point to Cape Crozier just over half a century
ago was accomplished in 30 minutes. We established our camp of
two pyramidal tents—the same design as used by Wilson—within
1 Km. of the penguins and awaited another helicopter to bring us a
small prefabricated hut. Prior visits like those of Wilson and, more
recently, Sir Edmund Hillary and New Zealand biologists from
Canterbury University had lasted only a few hours. We wished to
park ourselves near the birds and study them for several weeks
[fig. 1]. Although U.S. logistic support eliminated the lengthy journey over the ice shelf and pressure ridges, it had no effect on the
weather. A furious storm later forced us to abandon our tents and
shorten our visit.[3]

The aerial conquest of the continent emphasized by Albert P.
Crary has had an important effect not only on the type of research
that can now be accomplished in Antarctica, but also on the quality
of research. When I sailed to Antarctica on the 1,000-ton Royal Research Ship *John Biscoe* in 1947 with the Falkland Islands Dependencies Survey (now called British Antarctic Survey), it took us
over a month to reach our station at Hope Bay on the tip of the Ant-

[1] E. A. Wilson, *et al.,* in *Scott's Last Expedition,* II, comp. by Leonard Huxley (New York, 1913), 51-52.

[2] C. W. Parsons, "Penguin Embryos," *British Antarctic (Terra Nova) Expedition, 1910-13. Natural History Report,* Zoology, IV, 7 (London, 1934), 253-262.

[3] William J. L. Sladen, *et al.,* "Biotelemetry Studies on Penguin Body Tempera-tures," *Antarctic Journal of the United States,* I (July-August, 1966), 142-143.

FIGURE 1—Dr. William Sladen, aided by Robert Leresch (standing), attaches identification bands to Emperor Penguins in the rookery at Cape Crozier, Ross Island.

arctic Peninsula. We can now fly to McMurdo Station, Antarctica, in 27 flying hours or less from Washington, D.C.

In order to study the breeding biology of the Adelie Penguin, *Pygoscelis adeliae,* it was necessary in the late 1940's to spend the winter in Antarctica,[4] for no ships could penetrate the ice in early spring when the Adelies first walk into their breeding rookery. Now, thanks to U.S. air support, it is possible to be at the rookeries and ready for the penguins when they arrive. This illustrates a point that highlights the U.S. antarctic program and that of the New Zealanders with whom we collaborate in the Ross Sea area: it is now possible to get scientists to Antarctica in almost the same time it takes to get them to remote places in the Arctic. Antarctica is no longer an isolated continent. Experienced scientists can now visit their field teams and consult with their students on the spot with minimal delays. The quality of research and its potentials are thus enormously increased.

Mention should also be made of the latest triumph in logistic

[4] Sladen, "The Pygoscelid Penguins, 1, Methods of Study; 2, The Adelie Penguin," *Falkland Islands Dependencies Survey, Scientific Report No. 17* (London, 1958), p. 97.

support for scientists. We should add the winter flights of July and August, 1967, from Christchurch to McMurdo Station[5] as another highlight to Crary's paper. One of the main aims of the U.S. biological program in Antarctica is to find out more about the unique adaptations of antarctic life forms to their rigorous climatic environment. These winter flights, if they continue, will offer good opportunities for austral winter research by senior university scientists and their students at a time of year when they are most free from their academic responsibilities.

Closely related to improved logistics is improved technology, and antarctic biologists have been quick to exploit this in their research. In 1957 one of the first needs emphasized by the Panel on the Biological and Medical Sciences of the National Academy of Sciences' Committee on Polar Research, who planned the first year of post-IGY biology, was to build a biology laboratory at McMurdo Station. This was the first of its kind in Antarctica. Its sophisticated equipment and facilities for marine biology, microbiology, physiology, and later biochemistry provided the first direct support to nearby fieldwork.[6]

Three other aspects of improved technology, among many that have helped biologists in Antarctica, illustrate how sophisticated research has become since the early exploring days. These are marine biology, biotelemetry, and SCUBA diving. During the winter of Captain Scott's last expedition in 1911, Nelson writes about the painstaking marine biological work carried out on the sea ice of McMurdo Sound.

> After the sea had frozen over the general winter work was commenced. A hole was cut through the ice and a wall of ice blocks built round to afford some shelter from the wind. The hole had to be cut every day, freezing during the night to as much as two feet thick. . . . The labour entailed in keeping the holes open was considerable, and the time taken in this work very appreciably curtailed the time available for making collections.[7]

[5] John Hoshko, "Night Flight to Antarctica," *Antarctic Journal of the United States,* II (November-December, 1967), 261-264.

[6] Donald E. Wohlschlag, "The Biological Laboratory and Field Research Facilities at the U.S. McMurdo Station, Antarctica," *Polar Record,* XI (September, 1963), 713-718.

[7] E. W. Nelson, "Marine Biology—Winter Quarters," in *Scott's Last Expedition,* II, 335-388.

It is now possible to sit in a warm hut on the McMurdo sea ice and collect marine biological specimens (as has been shown by Donald E. Wohlschlag and his colleagues at Stanford University and others) in comparative comfort when outside temperatures may be as low as −70° F.

During the IGY Carl Eklund,[8] the scientific leader at Wilkes Station, was the first to use the technique of biotelemetry in the field. He inserted small radio transmitters into Adelie Penguin eggs and monitored by remote receiver the incubation temperature. It did not need to be done this way; in fact, more accurate temperatures could probably have been obtained by thermistor probes attached to a resistance bridge. But Eklund and the Office of Naval Research sponsoring his program reasoned that this new technique needed a trial. Biotelemetry devices were used again in Antarctica by Johns Hopkins University in December, 1965, to monitor, by surgical implant, the body temperatures of penguins;[9] but between times the technique had become one of the most important methods for study of movements and physiology of free-living animals throughout the world.

The third technological development, SCUBA diving, certainly did not originate in Antarctica like biotelemetry. In fact, the early explorers were closer to the mechanized era in Antarctica than to the concept that man could swim in a wet suit under the ice. Now, thanks to pioneers like Michael Neushul,[10] John Littlepage, Carleton Ray, Jacques S. Zaneveld, and an increasing band of biologists, this technique is commonplace and being used to unravel the mysteries of the underwater ecosystems in a way conventional and marine biological methods have never been able to do [fig. 2]. A study such as Ray's[11] on the underwater behavior of the Weddell Seal, where the SCUBA diver shares the same blow-hole and swims with the seals, is a very courageous approach to biological research.

I would like to conclude by expanding on Crary's remarks concerning the Antarctic Treaty. This treaty is an exciting one, for it

[8] C. R. Eklund and F. E. Charlton, "Measuring the Temperatures of Incubating Penguin Eggs," *American Scientist*, XLVII (March, 1959), 80-86.

[9] Sladen, "Biotelemetry Studies."

[10] M. Neushul, "Diving in Antarctic Waters," *Polar Record*, X (January, 1961), 353-358.

[11] Carleton Ray, "Social Behavior and Acoustics of the Weddell Seal," *Antarctic Journal of the United States*, II (July-August, 1967), 105-106.

FIGURE 2—Charles Galt, University of Washington, searches for organisms in the waters of McMurdo Sound off Hut Point.

not only insures international cooperation from the governmental level down to the individual scientist, but also, among other things, makes conservation a certainty. It puts an end to indiscriminate killing of antarctic animals. Measures have been agreed upon before any significant devastation to the flora and fauna has been done by man. This is an unusual approach in the history of mankind. Measures are usually taken in retrospect when a much-exploited species is near to extermination. Specially protected species and specially protected areas have been recommended by the Scientific Committee for Antarctic Research (SCAR),[12] and it seems probable that all member nations will agree on these.

Perhaps one of the main reasons for the success of the Antarctic Treaty is the fact that there are no important international vested

[12] "Report of the Fourth Antarctic Treaty Consultative Meeting, Santiago, Chile, 1966." *Polar Record*, XIII (May, 1967), 629-658.

interests in Antarctica. The commercial potentials of the antarctic seas are still untapped, but research from the commercial aspect (I am talking about seals, fish, and the abundant swarming shrimp called Krill, *Euphausia superba*) is being carried on intensively by several nations. At present, the United States is uninterested in this form of exploitation.

It is vital to the future of Antarctica and to the continued success of the Antarctic Treaty that the biologists, especially the marine biologists, continue their research on the antarctic seas and on the animals that are dependent on it. Good conservation and successful harvesting of manageable resources of the future must be founded on carefully planned and long-term studies on the almost inaccessible pack ice ecosystem, an ecological entity we know practically nothing about. This is where the U.S. genius for technology will excel in future antarctic research. It is my earnest desire, and I am sure that of my fellow scientists, that Antarctica will continue to prove, as it has already done in full measure, to be the best testing ground on earth for true international cooperation and international conservation.

SESSION III
Writing and Research on Antarctica

CHAIRMAN:

David M. Tyree

A 1925 graduate of the U.S. Naval Academy and a Rear Admiral since 1952, Rear Admiral Tyree was Commander, U.S. Naval Support Force, Antarctica, from April 1959 to November 1962. Since his retirement from active naval service in 1963, he has been engaged in polar studies and is affiliated with the Arctic Institute of North America.

The third session includes two papers by leaders of exploration in the Antarctic, a paper by an authority on the history of U.S. activity in the Antarctic, and comments by a colleague who is especially knowledgeable in the history of the administration of Operation Deep Freeze.

The United States Antarctic Service (USAS), under the command of Rear Admiral Richard E. Byrd, has specific plans for the geographical exploration and scientific appraisal of Antarctica. It reflected the awakening by the U.S. Government to the importance of the development of an antarctic program supported and coordinated by scientists and technicians. The USAS Expedition, 1939–41, established two principal bases: West Base, situated in the northeast corner of Ross Ice Shelf, under the command of Paul A. Siple, and East Base, situated in Marguerite Bay

*on the other side of the continent, under the command of
Richard B. Black.*

*Paul A. Siple's paper will be read by his long-time col-
league, F. Alton Wade, who collaborated with him in
writing it.*

WEST BASE OPERATIONS, UNITED STATES ANTARCTIC SERVICE, 1939–41

Paul A. Siple
F. Alton Wade

Selected from 600,000 candidates to be the Boy Scouts of America representative on Byrd's 1928-30 antarctic expedition, Dr. Siple has devoted the rest of his life to polar fieldwork, exploration, and study. He was chief biologist during Byrd's second expedition to Antarctica, 1933-35; commander of West Base during the U.S. Antarctic Service Expedition, 1939-41; senior War Department observer with *Operation Highjump,* 1946-47; and Scientific Station Leader of the Amundsen-Scott South Pole Station during IGY, 1957-58. From 1942 to August 1946 he was on active duty with the U.S. Army; from 1946 to 1963 he was military Geographer and Senior Advisor with the U.S. Army; and from 1963 to 1966 he was Scientific Attaché to the U.S. Embassies in Australia and New Zealand. Since 1966 he has been Special Scientific Advisor with the Department of the Army. [Dr. Siple died on November 25, 1968.]

Professor within the Department of Geosciences at Texas Technological College, Dr. Wade has done fieldwork in Antarctica from the time of his service as geologist on Byrd's second expedition to Antarctica, 1933-35, to his service as senior scientist of the Byrd Coast Survey Party, 1966-67. He has published many articles about geology and geoscience, coauthored textbooks on mineralogy and physical geology, and prepared studies for the Federal Government in glaciology and geology of the polar regions.

INTRODUCTION

The United States Antarctic Service (USAS) was conceived as a continuing project, and the aims and goals of the USAS Expedition set forth in the official orders to the commanding officer, Rear Admiral Richard E. Byrd, and signed by President Franklin D. Roosevelt were written with that fact in mind.[1] It is an amazing truth that, although the expedition was terminated at the end of its second austral summer (1941), the majority of its goals had been attained in addition to some that had not been included in the original plans. It is to the credit of the men who were stationed at East and West Bases and on shipboard and to the continued planning of their leaders in the field that this was so.

The USAS was conceived in haste, and, as a result, the plans, except for geographical exploration, were quite general and somewhat vague as stated in the official orders. To quote from one paragraph, "6. (e) The scientific program outlined by the National Research Council of the National Academy of Sciences shall form the basis for the scientific efforts at the bases."[2] This order became known to the expedition's senior scientist, F. Alton Wade, when the ships (the *North Star* and the *Bear*) were well on their way to New Zealand, last stop before Antarctica—a little late for high-level conferences.

Fortunately, planning for a third Byrd expedition was in an advanced stage at the time the USAS was formed. The prospectus of the scientific program that was prepared and submitted by Wade was the result of the recommendations of many scientific authorities who had been consulted. It was discussed at a meeting at the National Academy of Sciences on July 28, 1939, by representatives of Government scientific agencies, private institutions, and the USAS. No comments, criticisms, or suggestions concerning the scientific program other than at this meeting were communicated directly to Wade.

Program modifications and amendments originated in the field

[1] For a printed copy of Roosevelt's order of November 25, 1939, to Byrd, see National Archives, *Records of the United States Antarctic Service,* Preliminary Inventory No. 90 (Washington, 1955), pp. 15-18.

[2] *Ibid.,* p. 16.

as circumstances dictated. Some programs were curtailed because of incorrect instrumentation for polar environments, a result of haste in launching the entire operation. The time factor was responsible, also, for a crisis that developed when the Presidential orders were published aboard the *North Star* en route to Antarctica. The following paragraph in particular was not acceptable to the civilian scientists:

> 9. (c) As it is highly important that no journal or narrative of the enterprise, either partial or complete, should be published, without the authority and under the supervision of the Government of the United States, at whose expense this Service is undertaken, you will, before they reach the first port north of the Antarctic regions, require from every person under your command the surrender of all journals, diaries, memoranda, remarks, writings, charts, drawings, sketches, paintings, photographs, films, plates, as well as all specimens of every kind, collected or prepared during their absence from the United States.[3]

This provision was not known to the scientists when they signed on. As a matter of record, the orders had not been written when most of them agreed to join the expedition. They could visualize the complete loss of control of their data, specimens, etc., with the result of nothing to show for their efforts but an invaluable experience and a year of hardships. Most of them had professional advancement in mind. Surely, the pittances that they were paid were no inducements. Open rebellion resulted. They threatened to quit the expedition in New Zealand unless this paragraph were eliminated or at least drastically changed. Compromise was the solution, but the incident caused a lowering in the *esprit de corps* from which recovery was never complete. In fairness it might be said that the provisions of this paragraph were never enforced and that no one suffered professionally.

The USAS Expedition was the largest to go to Antarctica up to that time, and its accomplishments in the fields of exploration and scientific research far surpassed those of any previous expedition and have not been matched by any single expedition since that time.[4]

[3] *Ibid.*, p. 18.

[4] For USAS records in the custody of the National Archives, see Preliminary Inventory No. 90 noted in the first footnote. See also the papers of Paul A. Siple, Carl R. Eklund, and Capt. Harold E. Saunders in the Center for Polar Archives in the National Archives.

The truth of this rather astounding statement will become evident in the following summary of the accomplishments at West Base (Little America III) and on shipboard. To these must be added those numerous accomplishments of the men at East Base, which are summarized in an accompanying paper.

In the discussions that follow, the explorations from the U.S.S. *Bear* along the coast from Sulzberger Bay to Thurston Island are included because of their close relationships to those forays from Little America III and in the light of present-day activities in Byrd Land.

GEOGRAPHICAL EXPLORATION

In the orders to Admiral Byrd it was stated:

> 6. (c) The principal objective in the field is the delineation of the continental coast line between the meridians 72° W., and 148° W., and the consolidation of the geographical features of Hearst Land, James W. Ellsworth Land, and Marie Byrd Land. . . . Flights in this area should be made from the U.S.S. *Bear,* if practicable, . . . along the 75th, 101st, 116th, 134th, 150th, and 152nd meridians of West Longitude.[5]

As was to be expected, sea ice conditions prevented the *Bear*'s approaching the continent along the specified meridians. However, flights were made from the *Bear* during two cruises eastward from Little America III in late January and late February, 1940, and great sections of the unknown coast were photographed and mapped. Sulzberger Bay and the northern Ford Ranges, the Ruppert Coast, and the Hobbs Coast were mapped during the January flights; the Walgreen Coast, Thurston Island, and Eights Coast during the February flights. It is estimated that between 700 and 800 miles of new coastline were added to the map by these efforts. Relatively short gaps of unexplored coast remained on the map between 90° W. and 150° W.

It was suspected but not known at this time that West Antarctica was a separate entity and not a continuation of the East Antarctic Continent. That West Antarctica was an archipelago and not a land

[5] National Archives, Preliminary Inventory No. 90, p. 16.

mass of subcontinental proportions was not known because of the thick, continuous ice sheet that masks the underlying land. Subsequent investigations have proven the archipelagic nature of West Antarctica and the fact that the exploratory flights from the *Bear* resulted in the mapping of all but one of the northern coasts of the northernmost islands in this hitherto unknown section of the archipelago, a remarkable feat.

Most of the geographical exploration from Little America III was to have been by air, making use of the Condor aircraft for that purpose. When it became evident that the mighty snow cruiser could not fulfill its mission as a mobile base on the polar plateau, that unit was absorbed by the Little America III unit. Also, a single-engine Beechcraft on skis that was to have been used as a satellite plane from the snow cruiser became available for exploration from Little America III. Therefore, a greater amount of exploration by air in the coastal sectors was accomplished than had been anticipated, but at the cost of more southerly exploration.

Geographical exploration was conducted from Little America III during 1940 and early 1941 by means of the two aircraft and five field parties. The routes of the latter took them beyond the areas explored during the Byrd expeditions of 1929 and 1934, and the ground surveys were extended in Edward VII Peninsula and Byrd Land as far east as the Flood Range. Aerial surveying was extended eastward with major features as far east as 120° W. being photographed. These surveys extended and supplemented those made from the *Bear* in January, 1940. Because flights from the *Bear* approached the coast from the north and those by the land-based planes from the south, coverage and detail were greatly enhanced.

Supplemental to the authorized flights of exploration east of Little America III were three major flights west and southwest of that base. The major portion of the Ross Ice Shelf was observed and mapped. Previously unknown areas of disturbed ice were noted. Four hundred miles of the face of the Ross Ice Shelf were photographed. Of particular importance was the filling of the gap in the Transantarctic Mountains between the Beardmore and Liv Glaciers.

One secondary geographical objective was not attained: "6. (d) . . . the determination of the eastern extremity of the Queen Maud Range and the William Horlick Mountains and their relationship to the Sentinel Range."[6] This phase of the exploratory program was to have been the responsibility of the snow cruiser unit or reserved for operations in the second or third years of USAS activity.

SCIENTIFIC RESEARCH

The scientific program at Little America III included detailed observations and research in the following fields: auroral phenomena, bacteriology, botany, cosmic rays, glaciology, magnetism, medicine, meteorology, ornithology, paleontology, petrology, physiology, seismology, stratigraphy, structural geology, and zoology. Eleven trained scientists were responsible for carrying out the program at this western base. Only with the assistance of many volunteers from the group of technicians was it possible for the scientists to pursue their programs of research and produce maximum results.

The geographical location of Little America III was an excellent one from which to observe the Aurora Australis. The aurora observatory was manned continuously during the winter night when skies were clear, and 1,553 individual aurora were observed and recorded from April 1 to September 15, 1940. In order to determine the height of displays a second observatory was established some 15 miles from Little America III. During two periods in July, 1940, simultaneous photographs were taken from the two observatories of individual aurora. From the azimuth and vertical angle of the line of sight of each camera, altitudes could be calculated. The men who occupied the second observatory are to be highly commended since at times they were making observations when temperatures were in the −70's.

The biological investigations were extremely productive. Particularly is this true when it is realized that upon the shoulders of one man rested the responsibility for this phase of the program. The more important contributions to botany and zoology resulted from observations and collections made on sledge journeys to the Rockefeller Mountains and the Ford Ranges. Every member of every party was a collector and an observer, and their contributions supplemented those of the biologist who concentrated his efforts in the northern Ford Ranges. Specimens of seals, penguins, and flying birds

[6] *Ibid.,* p. 16.

that frequent the Bay of Whales were collected (some alive, some dead) for shipment to zoological gardens and museums. It is note-worthy that three specimens of the very rare Ross seal were collected at the Bay of Whales.

In the field of physiology three important investigations were carried out. One set of experiments was devised to determine the extent to which increased wind velocity increases human discomfort in a given degree of cold. Based upon the results of these experiments, the now well-known wind-chill index was devised. It has been used successfully in the development and use of clothing to be worn under various weather conditions in the polar and subpolar regions. The second and third physiological projects were designed to determine the degree of body acclimatization to cold. Observations began in Boston before sailing and were continued for 1 year, which took the subjects through the winter night and into the second summer. Definite changes in metabolism, red- and white-cell counts, skin and subcutaneous structures, blood-sugar levels, blood pressures, pulse and respiratory rates, and mental attitudes were noted. The degree of change of each varied from individual to individual, but all re-acted to life in the cold in the same general way. Apparently the human body does adapt to life in new environments by making specific basic changes.

Detailed experiments were conducted at Little America III to determine the physical aspects of shelf ice. These included: density variations with depth, rate of compaction, temperatures and tem-perature variations to depths of 41 meters, changes in the snow sur-face level, stratification and banding, and size and orientation of ice crystals at different depths. Similar observations and determinations had been made in valley glacier ice in lower latitudes, but never on shelf ice.

The program for the observation of cosmic rays consisted of three parts: (a) observations aboard ship, (b) continuous observa-tions at Little America III and observations during flights to various altitudes over the base, and (c) incidental observations of unusual phenomena. The trained specialists in this discipline confined their activities to observations aboard ship on the voyages to and from Antarctica and to the analysis of the data. At Little America III the meters were tended by various scientists. Records were obtained at the base for the period from April 27 through November 16, 1940.

The geophysicist restricted his activities largely to two fields: terrestrial magnetism and seismology. His observations in the first of these supplemented the many that had been taken by his predecessors on various expeditions in attempts to understand better the mysterious geomagnetic field. During the summer a seismic station was established on Mount Franklin in the Rockefeller Mountains. The seismographs were operated continuously for 41 days. From the records it would appear that Antarctica is a very stable, well-adjusted continent.

Geological observations were made by all of the major field parties. The Ford Mountains in Byrd Land were the object of an intensive geological survey that extended and supplemented the work of the 1934 field party in that area during the second Byrd expedition. Additional data and specimens were collected by parties operating in the Fosdick Mountains and as far east as the Flood Range. The reconnaissance survey of all peaks in the Rockefeller Mountains was completed.

Perhaps of greatest general importance was the meteorological program. Routine observations were begun on January 12, 1940, and were continued until the base was abandoned over a year later. Pilot balloons and radiosondes were used for upper air observations. A total of 219 successful pilot-balloon runs and 188 radiosonde ascents were made. Of the latter, 180 reached a minimum altitude of 6 kilometers; many of them attained greater altitudes. One unusual fact came to light from these observations. No tropopause existed during the winter in the lowest 12 kilometers of the atmosphere.

DISCUSSION

At the present time we are in the unique position of being able to evaluate the quality of many of the accomplishments of the USAS Expedition in these areas of Antarctica. During the past few years some of the activities in the Antarctic Research Program of the National Science Foundation have been concentrated in these same areas. Remapping of the coast from Cape Colbeck to the southern end of the Antarctic Peninsula and the mountainous areas to the south is in progress. Now there is available complete aerial photocoverage of the region, and about one-third of the ground control has been finished. When the map based upon 1940 observations and photographs is compared with the new preliminary maps, it is at once evident that the 1940 map was essentially correct in all major respects. Naturally, there were errors in positions of various features and in altitudes, but not serious ones, all things considered. These are to be expected in areas where there are no ground controls, no known positions to tie to.

Re-examination of the geology of the Ford Ranges and the Rockefeller Mountains has, with one major exception, confirmed the findings and interpretations of the USAS geologists. None of the major findings in the other branches of science investigated by men stationed at Little America III have been refuted or discredited.

It is interesting to note that we do not know, 27 years later, the answers to some of the more important questions concerning the western sector of Antarctica. What is its relationship to East Antarctica? Knowledge gained during and since the International Geophysical Year indicates that Byrd Land, including Edward VII Peninsula, is an archipelago. The individual insular masses have the thickness and other characteristics of continental masses. Were they torn from East Antarctica? Did they drift into their present positions? How are they related to the Antarctic Peninsula? The question concerning the relationship of the Sentinel-Heritage Ranges to the Transantarctic Mountains, the answer to which was requested in the Presidential orders for the USAS Expedition, has not been answered. Nor do we know their relationships to the islands of West Antarctica or the Antarctic Peninsula. Much remains to be done, but explorers of the future can be eternally thankful for the splendid and thorough groundwork done for them by the men of the United States Antarctic Service.

Thirty-three men were stationed at Little America III. Each one played an important role in the work of exploration and research that was carried out at or from that base. The combined efforts of all produced the gratifying results, and each is due his share of the credit. Personnel stationed at Little America III were:

Scientific Staff

Leonard M. Berlin, *cadastral engineer*
Arnold Court, *meteorologist*

Roy G. Fitzsimmons, *magnetician, seismologist*
Russell G. Frazier, *medical officer*
Ernest E. Lockhart, *physiologist*
Charles F. Passel, *geologist*
Jack E. Perkins, *biologist*
Paul A. Siple, *base leader, geographer*
F. Alton Wade, *senior scientist, geologist, glaciologist*
Lawrence A. Warner, *geologist*
Murray A. Wiener, *auroral observer*

Technicians

Adam Asman

Clay W. Bailey

Vernon D. Boyd

Jack Bursey

Raymond Butler

 Louis Colombo

Malcolm C. Douglass

Felix Ferranto

Walter R. Giles

 Harold P. Gilmour

Orville Gray

Clyde W. Griffith

Sigmund Gutenko

James McCoy

Richard S. Moulton

Raymond O'Connor

Theodore Petras

J. A. Reese

H. H. Richardson

Commander I. Schlossbach

Charles C. Shirley

Loran Wells

EAST BASE OPERATIONS, UNITED STATES ANTARCTIC SERVICE, 1939–41

Richard B. Black

Surveyor on Byrd's second expedition to Antarctica, 1933-35, and commander of East Base during the U.S. Antarctic Service Expedition, 1939-41, he was on active duty with the Navy during World War II. He retired from active naval service as a Rear Admiral in 1959. He served in various responsible positions in U.S. antarctic programs from 1954 to 1961.

East Base of the United States Antarctic Service (USAS) Expedition was established under my command in March, 1940, on a small rocky island in Marguerite Bay [fig. 1], 68°12′ S., 67°03′ W.—about 1,000 miles due south of Cape Horn. The island is connected to the mainland of the Antarctic Peninsula by a drifted snow slope leading to a quiescent glacier area of the continental ice. The island was eventually named Stonington Island after Stonington, Connecticut, which was the home port of the 47-foot sloop *Hero*. From that ship in 1820 Captain Nathaniel B. Palmer sighted land that was later proved to be a part of the Antarctic Continent. This proof was made by the members of East Base, who, following a strong supposition by John Rymill of the British Graham Land Expedition (1934-37) and a scholarly prognostication made from an analysis of Lincoln Ellsworth's photographs by W. L. G. Joerg that the feature was a peninsula and not an archipelago as surmised by Sir Hubert Wilkins, flew and sledged over the area from a point on the Weddell Sea coast

FIGURE 1—Looking southeast over Marguerite Bay. The "x" marks the area where East Base was built.

opposite East Base to 77° S. No straits or channels running westward through the peninsula were discovered.

The exploratory work by members of East Base was hampered, not by exceptionally low temperatures or a long winter night, but by extremely unfavorable weather during the season when exploration by flight (the base had one Condor for this purpose) and trail could be undertaken. Under conditions of light westerly winds, which were frequent, low clouds would lie for weeks on end against the western escarpment of the peninsula where the comparatively warm flow of air came in contact with the ice-covered mountains. When the general direction of the winds changed to easterly or southerly, bringing clear skies, it was necessary to seize the opportunity for a flight before the velocity at the base built up dangerously as the air poured down, williwaw fashion, from the mountain passes.

Including the test flights and the 16 exploratory and cache-laying flights we made, a total of only 94 flying hours was logged. This low figure dramatically emphasizes the preponderance of days with unfavorable weather conditions for flying in this region.

On August 6, 1940, a trail party of 10 men and 55 dogs started the ascent of Northeast Glacier to prospect for a feasible route across the high peninsular plateau down to the Weddell Sea. Rymill had judged that such a crossing would be next to impossible, but our aerial reconnaissance had indicated that a strong party might be able to negotiate the steep slopes and icefalls by doubling teams and using switchback techniques. The attempt was doomed to failure by the short periods of August daylight and by the arrival of a 100-mile-per-hour hurricane from the southeast, which caught the party in its camp (Mile High Camp) at an elevation of 5,500 feet on the night of August 9. One tent was demolished, and the others were kept standing only by repeated forays outside to replace tent pegs that had been cut out by the scouring drift snow, which also cut channels 3 feet deep around and under the tents. The mission was abandoned after 3 days, during which time the camp was in danger of being blown and cut from the exposed crest. The route made by the party was used later by the Weddell Coast Party in advancing its heavy loads to the far side of the plateau where a descent route was scouted and proven feasible for the start of its long southeasterly journey.

It had long been a dream of meteorologists to establish a station on a high antarctic plateau. Herbert G. Dorsey, Jr., the East Base weatherman, proposed such an outpost as a very important adjunct to the flight program. Consequently, on October 25, Lester Lehrke and Robert Palmer were placed at Mile High Camp with the equipment necessary for a weather station. They manned the station for 68 days, made 268 observations and 25 pilot-balloon soundings, and survived several severe blizzards.

On November 4, 1940, our first long flight was made across Marguerite Bay to the northern tip of "Alexander I Land." Charcot Island to the west was covered with haze and could not be seen, but it was determined that Rymill's "Rothschild Cape" was actually an island separated from "Alexander I Land" by a strait filled with sea ice holding many trapped icebergs. The flight proceeded south, mapping the unknown western coast of "Alexander I Land" (including the southern part of the strait mentioned above, and still showing the telltale icebergs), then southeasterly to an intersection with George VI Sound at 70°13′ S., 68° W. The sound was filled with a creamy white undercast that contrasted with the darker snow-covered highlands and thereby revealed the definite westerly trend of the sound.

We continued southeasterly, and once abreast of the Batterbee Mountains we made our first important discovery. Far to the east, appearing over the high and almost featureless spine of the Antarctic Peninsula, was a large double-mountain feature; and well to the north of it was a high mountain range. The large double mountain was originally called Mounts Ernest and Dorothy Gruening, since Gruening had done so much to put this expedition in the field; later it was named Mount Andrew Jackson by the U.S. Board on Geographic Names. Its imposing height of 13,750 feet was observed more closely during the flight of December 30, 1940.

The mountain range to the north of this double-mountain feature we judged to be the Eternity Range. However, we were wrong. About 2 years ago it was agreed between British and U.S. authorities that the mountain range named "Wakefield" by Rymill in 1936 is the same as the Eternity Range (69°46′ S., 64°34′ W.), named by Ellsworth in 1935. Negotiations are now being pursued with the U.S. Board on Geographic Names to assign a suitable name to the still-nameless range we saw. It spans latitude 71° S. between longitudes 63°-64° W. for over 30 miles.

In addition to numerous short sledging journeys to scout routes, train personnel and dogs, and advance supplies for future operations, there were two major trail journeys. One was made by the Southern Party under Finn Ronne; the other was made by the Weddell Coast Party under Paul H. Knowles.

The Southern Party, consisting of Ronne, Carl R. Eklund, J. Glenn Dyer, Joseph Healy, and Lytton Musselman, left East Base on November 6, 1940. Accompanying them to help advance loads for a few days was a supporting party (Knowles and Donald C. Hilton), which returned to base from the Wordie Ice Shelf. When the main Southern Party reached the high eastern flank of George VI Sound, they divided into two groups—Ronne and Eklund traveling southwest while the three others, under Dyer, headed southeast. Ronne and Eklund made a remarkable march of about 1,100 nautical miles in 84 days. They found that George VI Sound swings westward to join the Bellingshausen Sea (an extension of the south Pacific Ocean) and thereby proved that "Alexander I Land" is actually an island some 250 miles long and 150 miles wide. (It has been renamed

Alexander Island.) Its upthrust as a gigantic horst had produced one of the earth's largest fault features—George VI Sound. Ronne and Eklund's ground-control work later helped the two exploratory mapping flights in that direction.

Dyer and his companions sledged in a general southeasterly direction to the foothills north of what we then thought to be the Eternity Range. After making detailed surveys and collecting many rock specimens in this area, they returned to base, arriving on December 11, 1940, after 35 days on the trail.

The Weddell Coast Party, consisting of Knowles, Hilton, and Harry Darlington, III, left East Base on November 18, 1940. They picked up supplies previously cached on the peninsular plateau and descended a heavily crevassed glacier to the Weddell Sea. They then sledged southward, traveling sometimes on the wide piedmont ice and sometimes on the sea ice, until they reached 71°51′ S., 60°40′ W., and turned back to the base. They reached East Base on January 17, 1941, having covered about 684 nautical miles in 59 days. Their ground-control work served the long Weddell coast flight of December 30, 1940, and several shorter flights of earlier dates. Rock specimens were taken from 22 sites by Knowles, the base geologist, and Hilton and Darlington made numerous astronomic fixes and surveyed prominent features of the coastline and interior.

Following the flight of November 4, 1940, impossible weather kept the plane grounded for 45 frustrating days except for two short logistic flights. The first of these (November 12) was to place gasoline, man-food, dog-food, and kerosene for the Primus stoves at a point on the shelf ice in George VI Sound near the Batterbee Mountains (known as the Batterbee Cache, 71°45′ S., 67°50′ W.); the second (November 16) was to take additional supplies to the Southern Party at the cache on the Wordie Ice Shelf (the cache and its pole and flag marker had been lost in winter storms). Interior land routes marked on aerial photographs were also delivered since it was expected that the sea ice in Marguerite Bay would be broken up by the time of Ronne and Eklund's return.

On December 20, 1940, the weather was finally clear, and an attempt was made to fly the planned Weddell coast exploration flight. However, the plane had not completed the transit across the peninsula when clouds could be seen forming in the "Wakefield

Mountains" area ahead. We returned to base, circling for a long time to burn gasoline in order to make the landing safer. Soon after landing a complete overcast closed in.

The flight party took off in the Condor on December 22 for a mapping flight in the direction of the Ronne and Eklund sledging party and the Bellingshausen Sea. This was the only long flight I did not make; I had injured my leg during a fall while on skis. Visibility over much of the course was obscured by heavy undercast, but coastal mountains and the open sea west of Ronne's position to about 84° W. were seen and mapped.

Another flight was made on December 28. The plan was to fly due south from the Batterbee Cache if possible; the alternative was to fly west in George VI Sound to and beyond Ronne's position. Low clouds in the south made the alternative necessary, but much valuable aerial mapping was done on both sides of the sound to about 78° W. Sims Island was discovered and named after the East Base medical officer, Lieutenant Lewis S. Sims; a group of nunataks was discovered south of the coast and was named for chief pilot Ashley C. Snow. Many high mountains were seen on the horizon to the south and southwest.

The last extended flight was made on December 30. A course was laid down George VI Sound until a low pass through the eastern escarpment, remembered from previous flights, was found. This was followed to a point just south of Mount Andrew Jackson where a great glacier valley appeared to descend to the Weddell Sea. Long before reaching the sea, a band of dark water sky revealed the presence of open water. We intersected the coast at 72°32′ S., 60°23′ W., where the open water was seen to be a shore lead 2 or 3 miles wide running north and south as far as we could see from this point. The pass to the sea has been named Gruening Glacier by the U.S. Board on Geographic Names.

The flight had to be terminated with a photographic circle at about 74°37′ S., 61°15′ W., where a coastal mountain had the shape of a tricorn hat of the American Continental Army. It was named Mount Tricorn. Not clear in the photographs, but clearly visible to the crew, the chain of massive mountains that had been to starboard since the intersection with the coast went on southerly in somewhat diminishing height until lost in the distant haze at about 77° S. Increasing haze around the plane's position and some worry about the amount of remaining gasoline dictated that we return from this point, leaving the solution of the greatest coastal mystery left on earth to the later Ronne Antarctic Research Expedition, 1946-48.

It must be mentioned that this flight was made 8 days after the Weddell Coast Party had reached its outward limit and had turned to return to base. It was therefore a flight that could expect no ground support in case of a forced landing. The men aboard had this fact clearly brought to their attention when both engines stopped during the descent from the peninsula to the Weddell Sea due to running too long on one of the cabin gas tanks. The engines fired again in 20 or 30 seconds when a new tank was cut in, but this was a long time—there is no more complete silence this side of the grave.

At the conclusion of flight operations, members of East Base had discovered and mapped 1,600 miles of previously unknown coastline (probably more than any whole expedition to the Antarctic, before or since) and had observed roughly 250,000 square miles of new land and sea areas. In addition, by sledge and flight, we had proved the insularity of "Alexander I Land" and the peninsularity of the Antarctic Peninsula, as mentioned above.

On their return journey, Ronne and Eklund reached the Batterbee Cache on January 6, 1941, with only 7 of their 15 dogs remaining. The dogs' paws had been lacerated by the sharp freeze-and-thaw crust, which is a summer plague in this region. Canvas and leather boots were tried on the dogs' paws; but these worried the dogs, and they did additional damage with their teeth. The men had carried, lashed to the sledges, as many as two or three wounded dogs, but, as their power dwindled, they had to destroy one after another to enable them to reach the cache where food and fuel were stored. Having radioed to the base their condition and the necessity for a 10-day stop at the cache to heal the dogs' paws, their hand generator went out of commission. We did not hear them again. We felt certain that the receiver was functioning and therefore continued to transmit blind bulletins at regularly scheduled times covering plans to relieve them by air. On January 19, the first day with flying weather since our last message from them, the left ski of the plane dropped through a crevasse bridge while trying to take off. The tip of the heavy wood and metal ski was sheared off by the propeller 2 feet from its end, and the lower left wing was seriously crumpled. Repair work started at once, and a strong surface party of four men started preparing to sledge to a hopeful meeting with Ronne and Eklund on their aerially charted, but never traveled, inland route. The two parties met in Neny Trough, only about 30 miles from the base. This was on January 27, and the happy event signaled the safe return of the last of the field parties.

Although the personnel of East Base and their equipment were selected primarily to achieve the geographical reconnaissance of unknown or slightly known regions, men and instruments were also included to attack the problems of science usually associated with polar expeditions.

Dorsey recorded barometric pressure, wind direction and velocity, temperature, humidity, precipitation, and a variety of visual observations of sky phenomena. He took 1,200 synoptic observations, 370 pilot-balloon soundings, aerometeorograph records during flights, tide data for the summer period, and air samples; and he completed a series of radiation measurements. He also planned the program of Mile High Camp.

One hundred and twenty-three geological outcroppings were studied by Knowles. The peninsula is composed of a central core of massive igneous rocks flanked on the east and west sides by metamorphics varying from slates to gneisses. The igneous rocks compare in composition with those of the southern Andes of South America. Dikes, both basic and acidic in character, are found throughout the entire region in close association with the igneous rocks. Well-defined, low-angle, stratified, fossiliferous, sedimentary rocks occur in massive outcrops along the eastern and southern margins of Alexander Island. These rocks are composed of mudstones, conglomerates, and graywackes in which is included carbonaceous material derived from the trees of a past age. The general topography of the region of East Base is that of a mountainous glaciated land in the early stages of glacial erosion.

Herwil M. Bryant and Eklund carried on a comprehensive program of botanical and zoological investigations. Dyer, Ronne, and Hilton engaged in aerial and surface survey work and made a series of magnetic observations. Elmer L. Lamplugh, Earle B. Perce, and Howard T. Odom stood receiving watches on transmissions from Washington, D.C., to determine over a long period of time the frequencies best suited for various types and times of communication. Unfortunately, these radio records were lost when the sledge upon which they were packed plunged into the sea from the 400-foot cliff of Mikkelsen Island (now Watkins Island) during the emergency air evacuation of the base.

In addition to their scientific work, most of the above men engaged in long journeys of discovery during which each cooperated with the others in collecting specimens and data in fields other than their own. Many have published their findings in scientific journals, and investigators at home universities have assisted in refining their data for further publication. The call of practically every man into the armed services soon after his return to the United States resulted in a dearth of published material from the USAS Expedition. It is to be hoped that, with the assistance of the facility we dedicate today, many will find opportunity to prepare further work for publication.

The emergency air evacuation of East Base was necessary since the easterly winds were not of sufficient strength to clear the winter ice from Marguerite Bay at a time when thaw pools and rotting ice would have made the clearance relatively easy. The *North Star* and the *Bear* arrived off the bay in mid-February, 1941, but could not force their way in. To conserve fuel they moved north to ride at anchor in Andersen Harbor, but the *Bear* made weekly cruises to observe conditions nearer the base. By mid-March the thaw pools that had formed were covered with 6 inches of new ice, and heavy snowfall presaged the early return of winter.

The growing emergency was heightened by the threat of United States involvement in World War II, already raging in Europe. Messages from the USAS Executive Committee in Washington revealed that there was worry on this score in the highest circles of the Government. Almost hourly radiotelephone conversations were held between the base and Captain Richard Cruzen of the *Bear* and Captain Isak Lystad of the *North Star*. Rear Admiral Richard E. Byrd, commanding officer of the expedition, was in Washington and Boston and had ordered Captain Cruzen to assume the position of second-in-command for the purpose of relieving the two bases. West Base had already been evacuated successfully.

On March 20 the *North Star* sailed for Punta Arenas, Chile, to take on food for a year and a full load of fuel and to drop off most of the men of West Base so that she would be able, upon returning, to take better advantage of any easing of the ice. The next day the *Bear* was able to get to an anchorage near Mikkelsen Island. It was seen from the crow's-nest that there was a possible landing area for the repaired East Base Condor on the snowfield topping the ice-covered island. By radiophone it was decided that only personnel and records would be evacuated in two flights.

At 5:30 A.M. on March 22, 1941, with Snow and Perce at the controls and with 12 men crowded into the cabin on top of their records and emergency equipment, the Condor took off after a long and bumpy run and headed for Mikkelsen Island, 120 miles away. At 7:16 A.M. those of us remaining at East Base heard the tooting of the *Bear*'s siren signifying that the plane had landed safely.

While the two pilots were returning, several last-minute details were carried out to completely close the base. The most utterly disagreeable was the humane destruction of the 69 huskies who could not be left to starve and for whom there was no daylight time for a third flight.

FIGURE 2—The emergency landing field on top of Mikkelsen Island, taken as the second evacuation flight circled for a landing. Note the landing track of the first flight, the trail to the 400-foot cliff, and the U.S.S. *Bear* in the circle.

Snow and Perce landed at about 10:30 A.M. and an hour later tried to take off with the remaining 12 men and their gear. The surface had softened, however, and they were unable to make it until the load had been lightened by throwing out hundreds of pounds of food, clothing, and emergency equipment. At 12:15 noon the second attempt was made. The plane took to the air after an interminable run of 1 minute, 10 seconds, and after getting on a very rough section of the glacier. This roughness possibly helped her to bounce into the air. All hands were aboard the *Bear* by twilight, after having descended the cliff of Mikkelsen Island on lines erected by Paul A. Siple, leader of West Base, and some of his men and members of the ship's company [fig. 2].

Every man at East Base had volunteered for the last flight. The selection was made on the basis of the most needed skills in case of a second year at the base, except that one badly needed man was evacuated first for medical reasons. The following men were on the first flight: Harry Darlington, III; Hendrick Dolleman; J. Glenn Dyer; Joseph Healy; Archie C. Hill; Donald C. Hilton; Anthony J. L. Morency; Howard T. Odom; Robert Palmer; William Pullen; Charles W. Sharbonneau; and Clarence E. Steele (Ashley C. Snow and Earle B. Perce, pilots). Those on the second flight were: Richard B. Black, East Base leader; Herwil M. Bryant; Arthur J. Carroll; Zadick Collier; Herbert G. Dorsey, Jr.; Carl R. Eklund; Paul H. Knowles; Elmer L. Lamplugh; Lester Lehrke; Lytton Musselman; Finn Ronne; and Lewis S. Sims (Snow and Perce, pilots).

WRITING AND RESEARCH ON UNITED STATES EXPLORATION IN ANTARCTICA

Kenneth J. Bertrand

Professor of geography and Chairman of the Department of Geography at The Catholic University of America since 1946, Dr. Bertrand became an authority on the history of U.S. exploration in Antarctica while serving as a geographer in the Office of Geography, Department of the Interior, 1943-46. He has been a member of the Advisory Committee on Antarctic Names since 1948 and its chairman since 1963. He has written a history of U.S. exploration in Antarctica, published as a *Special Publication* by the American Geographical Society in 1971.

I. FUNDAMENTAL PROBLEMS

Since this conference marks the opening of the Center for Polar Archives, it is my intention in this paper to emphasize the source materials for the history of U.S. exploration in Antarctica. I will cover the period up to 1948, for that year marks the end of an era. Later research and exploration were related to the International Geophysical Year (IGY), 1957-58, and to post-IGY work, which was and is on an entirely different scope.

As we learned this morning from Henry M. Dater's paper, U.S. interests in the Antarctic have been of two types, commercial and scientific. Anyone delving into the history of these two activities is confronted with two different sets of problems. The commercial activity was almost entirely confined to hunting elephant seals for their oil and fur seals for their skins. This activity extended from 1775 to 1913, but most of it occurred in the first quarter of the nineteenth century. Information about the geographical exploration and discoveries of the sealers is scanty, widely scattered, and hard to find. Trying to piece together an account of their accomplishments is much like trying to put together a jigsaw puzzle with half the pieces missing.

The first U.S. scientific exploring expedition to the Antarctic was the Wilkes Expedition, officially the United States Exploring Expedition, during parts of 1839 and 1840. The most extensive scientific exploration by Americans has taken place in the twentieth century, especially since 1928. In dealing with the scientific exploring expeditions, one is confronted first of all with a great mass of material from which it is necessary to select the essential facts. Secondly, the material is widely scattered, and the researcher cannot be sure that he has seen it all.

Regardless of the era, three kinds of source materials provide information on U.S. antarctic exploration. First are books and periodicals containing firsthand accounts of activities. Second are newspaper reports. Third are unpublished manuscript materials, such as logbooks, journals, diaries, maps, sketches, and correspondence. Photographs of various kinds are part of the records of the twentieth-century expeditions.

II. AMERICAN SEALERS

A. Published Works

Initially, sealing was carried on in subantarctic waters, but as early as 1793 two vessels from New Haven, Connecticut, the brig *Nancy* and the brigantine *Polly,* crossed the Antarctic Convergence to reach the island of South Georgia. The discovery of the South Shetland Islands in 1819 by the British sea captain, William Smith, led to several years of intensive activity in that area, including cruises across Bransfield Strait to the Antarctic Peninsula by U.S. and British sealers.

Four American sealing captains, Charles H. Barnard, Amasa

Delano, Edmund Fanning, and Benjamin Morrell, Jr., wrote books describing their exploits.[1] Diaries or memoirs of at least three contemporaries who participated in sealing voyages have been published.[2] Only Fanning and Morrell deal with antarctic discoveries, and the latter has been widely discredited, perhaps unjustly. An excellent account of the hunting of both fur and elephant seals, stripped of all the adventurous narrative of the old sealing captains, is the often neglected work of Alonzo Howard Clark.[3] At the time he wrote, Clark was able to obtain statements from men still living who had participated in the early nineteenth-century sealing voyages. No one interested in U.S. activity in the South Shetlands should fail to read the book by the British sealing captain, James Weddell.[4]

Later U.S. writers, such as Edwin Swift Balch, William Herbert Hobbs, Lawrence Martin, John R. Spears, and Edouard A. Stackpole, have summarized the work of the sealing captains, adding newly discovered information of their own.[5] Hobbs and Martin were so in-

[1] Charles H. Barnard, *A Narrative of the Suffering and Adventures of Captain Charles H. Barnard, in a Voyage Round the World, During the Years 1812, 1813, 1814, 1815, and 1816* (New York, 1829); Amasa Delano, *Narrative of Voyages and Travels in the Northern and Southern Hemispheres* (Boston, 1817); Edmund Fanning, *Voyages Round the World* (New York, 1833); and Benjamin Morrell, Jr., *A Narrative of Four Voyages to the South Sea, North and South Pacific Ocean, . . . From the Year 1822 to 1831* (New York, 1832).

[2] Joel Root, "Narrative of a Sealing and Trading Voyage in the Ship Huron, from New Haven, Around the World, September, 1802, to October, 1806," *Papers of the New Haven Colony Historical Society*, V (New Haven, 1894), 149-171; Thomas R. Trowbridge, "The Diary of Mr. Ebenezer Townsend, Jr., the Supercargo of the Sealing Ship 'Neptune,' on her Voyage to the South Pacific and Canton," *Papers of the New Haven Colony Historical Society*, IV (New Haven, 1888), 1-115; and T. R. Trowbridge, ed., *Grandfather's Voyage Around the World in the Ship Betsey, 1799-1801* (New Haven, 1895).

[3] Alonzo Howard Clark, "The Antarctic Fur-Seal and Sea-Elephant Industry," in George B. Goode, *The Fisheries and Fishery Industries of the United States* (Washington, 1887). Published as S. Misc. Doc. 124, 47 Cong., 1 sess., Serial 2002, pp. 400-467.

[4] James Weddell, *A Voyage Towards the South Pole, Performed in the Years 1822-24* (London, 1825).

[5] Edwin Swift Balch, *Antarctica* (Philadelphia, 1902), pp. 75-113; Balch, "Stonington Antarctic Explorers," *Bulletin of the American Geographical Society*, XLI (August, 1909), 473-492; William Herbert Hobbs, "The Discoveries of Antarctica Within the American Sector, as Revealed by Maps and Documents," *Transactions of the American Philosophical Society*, New Series, XXXI, Pt. 1 (Philadelphia, January, 1939), 1-71; Lawrence Martin, "Antarctica Discovered by a Connecticut Yankee, Captain Nathaniel Brown Palmer," *The Geographical Review*, XXX (October, 1940), 529-552; John R. Spears, *Captain Nathaniel Brown Palmer, an Old-Time Sailor of the Sea* (New York, 1922); and Edouard A. Stackpole, *The Sea-Hunters* (Philadelphia, 1953), pp. 181-236 and 355-368.

tent on magnifying the discoveries of Nathaniel B. Palmer that they neglected the equally important efforts of some of his contemporaries. The latest and most complete account of the discoveries of U.S. sealers in the South Shetlands is based on the logbook of Captain John Davis of New Haven aboard the ship *Huron*.[6]

James Eights of Albany, New York, sailing aboard the brig *Annawan* in the combined sealing and exploring expedition sent out by Captain Fanning and his associates, 1829-31, was the first U.S. scientist to visit the Antarctic. He made significant contributions to scientific knowledge by writing seven papers. Because they were published in journals with limited circulation, Eights' work was generally neglected; however, almost a century later three different papers were written in appreciation of his work.[7] One of his papers is recognized as the earliest scientific description of the South Shetlands.[8]

B. Newspaper Accounts

From an early date it was general practice for newspapers published in U.S. port cities to carry a column of marine news, noting among other things the arrivals and departures of vessels. In the case of arrivals, interesting incidents during the voyage or news from ports that had been visited were sometimes reported. This was occasionally true of sealing vessels arriving from "the South Seas" or "New South Shetland." A careful examination of marine columns of papers published from March to June in the home ports of sealers has disclosed significant information concerning numerous sealing voyages. Records of customhouses sometime suggest the possibility of newspaper accounts, and the marine notices, in turn, have led to customhouse papers that have supplied further information about a

[6] Stackpole, *The Voyage of the Huron and the Huntress* (Mystic, Connecticut, 1955).

[7] W. T. Calman, "James Eights, A Pioneer Antarctic Naturalist," *Proceedings of the Linnean Society of London*, sess. 149, pt. 4 (November 3, 1937), 171-184; John M. Clarke, "The Reincarnation of James Eights, Antarctic Explorer," *The Scientific Monthly*, II (February, 1916), 189-202; and Lawrence Martin, "James Eights' Pioneer Observation and Interpretation of Erratics in Antarctic Icebergs," *Bulletin of the Geological Society of America*, LX (January, 1949), 177-181.

[8] James Eights, "Description of a new Crustaceous Animal found on the Shores of the South Shetland Islands, with Remarks on their Natural History," *Transactions of the Albany Institute*, II (Albany, 1833-52), 53-69.

particular voyage. In some cases interesting reports in the marine columns were followed by regular news stories in a subsequent issue. It is impossible to review any of these here, but they contain descriptions of the South Shetlands, reports of collections of mineral and plant specimens, and tantalizing remarks, such as, "The manuscript chart made by Mr. Hampton Stewart, is an instructive addition to geography, and ought to be incorporated into the charts of the globe."[9] Boston and New York papers are particularly fruitful sources for such reports, and often they were copied in *Niles' Weekly Register*. Perhaps much was brought home that was not reported. Although Samuel L. Mitchill, prominent New York physician and well known in early scientific circles, received some of this material and reported on it, its whereabouts is now unknown. The fate of specimens given to Samuel Topliff (who operated a news service in Boston that specialized in marine and commercial news) and displayed at Merchants' Hall in Boston is also unknown.[10] Unfortunately, there was at that time in the United States no organization or agency that systematically gathered and recorded such data. As a result, little use was made of them at the time, and most of the material was subsequently lost.

C. Manuscript Material

The papers of at least three persons who played important roles as antarctic sealing captains are available to scholars. The letters and business papers of Captain Fanning are in the library of the American Geographical Society of New York. The papers of Alexander S. and Nathaniel B. Palmer are in the Manuscript Division of the Library of Congress. The Palmer papers are much more complete than

[9] *New-York Gazette and General Advertiser*, May 16, 1821, p. 2. *See also* "Southern Thule," *New-York Gazette and General Advertiser*, May 22, 1821, p. 2. Both articles were reprinted in *Niles' Weekly Register*, XX, No. 15 (Whole No. 509) (Baltimore, June 9, 1821), 237-238.

[10] John Torrey, "Description of a New Species of Usnea, from New South Shetland," *The American Journal of Science*, VI No. 1 (1823), 104-106. This article contains a copy of the letter from Mitchill that accompanied specimens he sent to Torrey. *See also* [*New York*] *Columbian for the Country*, June 11, 1821; and *New England Palladium and Commercial Advertiser*, Boston, June 19, 1821. Articles in these issues reported the arrival in Boston of the ship *O'Cain* and the fact that Captain Jonathan Winship gave Topliff ". . . several kinds of curious stones, shells, minerals and fossil coal. . . ."

the Fanning papers and contain the logbooks of the sloop *Hero* (1820-21), the brig *Alabama Packet* (1821-23), and the schooner *Penguin* (1829-31). The logbook of the *Hero* records Nathaniel Palmer's cruise across Bransfield Strait from the South Shetlands to the shore of the Antarctic Peninsula in November, 1820. From the log of the *Penguin,* which sailed in company with the *Annawan* in 1829 and 1830, something can be inferred regarding James Eights' activities, including a march across the foot of a glacier.

In addition to the three Palmer logbooks, the logbooks from five other sealing voyages in the South Shetlands in the 1820's have been located.[11] The most informative is that of the *Huron,* in which Captain Davis made very complete entries, including remarks about vessels he encountered while cruising in his shallop *Cecilia* and about the goings and comings of other sealers who shared the anchorage in Yankee Harbor. In Davis' logbook for February 7, 1821, is recorded the earliest documented landing on the Antarctic Continent. On a cruise in the *Cecilia,* looking for seals, he sailed south from Low Island to put men ashore briefly in the vicinity of Hughes Bay.

Working with Davis was Captain Christopher Burdick in the schooner *Huntress* of Nantucket. He, too, recorded the activities of other sealers, and from his logbook we learn of Captain Robert Johnson's cruise along the west side of the Antarctic Peninsula as far as 66° S. in January, 1821. The brig *Hersilia,* in January and February, 1820, was the first U.S. vessel to visit the South Shetland Islands. The event is recorded in the logbook kept by first mate Elof Benson, who described the approach, arrival, and departure of the brig. However, for most of the time that the *Hersilia* lay at anchor in New Plymouth, the small embayment at the west end of Livingston Island, there are no entries.

[11] Alexander O. Vietor, "New Light on the Activities of American Sealing Vessels in the South Shetland Islands and Antarctica, 1819-1822," in Geography and Map Division, Special Libraries Association, *Bulletin* (December, 1956), pp. 5-9. Logbooks for the following vessels are listed in this article: the schooner *Huntress,* August 4, 1820-June 10, 1821 (property of Edouard A. Stackpole, Editor, *The Inquirer and Mirror,* Nantucket); the ship *Huron,* January 18, 1821-April 27, 1822 (property of Alexander O. Vietor, Map Curator, Yale University Library, New Haven, Conn.); the brig *Hersilia,* January 11-May 20, 1820, and the brig *Catharina,* July 30, 1820-May 11, 1821 (both logbooks in one binding, property of Mrs. Theodore Krueger, Stratford, Conn.; the Yale University Library and the Mystic Seaport Library, Mystic, Conn., have microfilm copies); and the schooner *Adventure,* August 10-November 22, 1821 (property of Mrs. Krueger).

Even the most complete logbook requires some interpretation in matters of longitude, compass bearings, dates, and geographic nomenclature. Although the sealers were remarkable navigators by dead reckoning, their chronometers were not very accurate, and the recorded longitude is as much as 5 to 8 degrees in error in the South Shetlands. Consider the problem of making celestial observations from the pitching deck of a vessel such as the 44-ton, 47-foot *Hero*. Yet latitudes obtained from such readings were generally fairly accurate. In some cases it is difficult to determine exact positions from recorded bearings because one cannot always be sure of the object being sighted. In some cases the problem can be solved by rotating an entire set of bearings, indicating an apparent disregard for magnetic declination, which in the 1820's in the South Shetlands was about 25° E.

When it is important to determine the exact calendar date of a landfall or landing, it must be recognized that the sealers kept their logs by what mariners then called the sea day. It began at noon, local time, which was determined when the sun was at meridian. It did not begin at midnight. Therefore, it was 12 hours ahead of civil time. For example, today is September 8, but if we were at sea and reckoning time by the method used by the early nineteenth-century mariners, September 9 would have begun this noon. The day was divided into three 8-hour watches, designated first, middle, and latter.

Fitting sealers' descriptions of unnamed landmarks to known features is often difficult. Recent research, mostly by Brian Roberts of the Antarctic Place Names Committee of the Permanent Committee on Geographic Names of the United Kingdom, has restored or retained sealers' names for almost all physical features on the latest maps of the South Shetlands. However, in some cases there was no agreement among the sealers regarding a particular name. In other cases the British had one name and the Americans another; for example, Smith Island, which the Americans called Monroe Island. Sealers' terminology was also different from modern usage in some respects. They invariably referred to glaciers as icebergs and to icebergs as ice islands.

A variety of manuscript material in the custody of the Government contains information relating to the sealers. Among these are records of customhouses, including crew lists, inbound cargo manifests, in some cases outbound cargo manifests, and ship registration papers. These records are in the National Archives Building[12] or in the Federal Records Center in Waltham, Massachusetts. The sealers sailed from New York; New Haven and Stonington, Connecticut; Westerly, Rhode Island; and Nantucket, New Bedford, Boston, and Salem, Massachusetts. In the middle of the nineteenth century, whalers from New London, Connecticut, made a specialty of hunting elephant seals on Kerguelen and Heard Islands.

The crew lists show that the men who officered the sealing vessels were a closely knit group with third mates moving up through successive promotions to the command of a ship. Affidavits by the captains to U.S. consular agents in foreign ports regarding desertions and deaths in various places help to date and place vessels in the absence of logbooks. Not infrequently, these dates do not correspond exactly with dates given in later memoirs by aging mariners, although there is sufficient supporting evidence to corroborate the bulk of the testimony.

Ship registration papers discount the supposition by some writers that secrets were part of the sealer's stock in trade.[13] Most sealing vessels were owned by several men, sometimes by as many as 8 or 10. Not infrequently a man was part owner in vessels belonging to different fleets. There are instances of Salem men owning shares in Stonington vessels. This practice was a form of insurance in that it spread the risk, but it made keeping secrets rather difficult.

There are several other kinds of Federal records in the National Archives that supply information about sealing voyages. Among these are letters received by the Department of State,[14] especially

---

[12] Records of some customhouses for the early nineteenth century are among French Spoilation Claims, Record Group 36, Records of the Bureau of Customs, National Archives. Hereafter records in the National Archives will be cited as RG ——, NA.

[13] Report of J. N. Reynolds on the Pacific Ocean and Its Islands and Coasts, September 24, 1828, RG 45, Naval Records Collection of the Office of Naval Records and Library, NA. On pages [18] and 19 of the report, Reynolds wrote: "In the history of the Seal trade, Secrecy in what they know has been deemed a part, and a very important part, too, of their capital. There is nothing more common at this time, than that Islands are frequented for animal Fur, and their positions known to no one on board but the Captain; and when an Island is discovered, the observations are made and noted down by the Captain in his private journal." E. S. Balch, on pages 109 and 110 of his book *Antarctica*, quoted at length from Reynolds, including the above. These sources were partly responsible for later writers emphasizing the importance of secrecy.

[14] See, for instance, Jeremy Robinson to John Quincy Adams, November 15, 1819, Vol. 5, p. 53, in Despatches from Special Agents, RG 59, General Records of the Depart-

while John Quincy Adams was Secretary since it was at that time that the South Shetland Islands were discovered.

Matthew Fontaine Maury, Superintendent of the Depot of Charts and Instruments and of the Naval Observatory and Hydrographical Office from 1842 to 1861, became convinced of the importance of exploration and research in Antarctica as a means of understanding world climate. A century before IGY he advocated an international cooperative effort in antarctic exploration. When he failed to convince the Secretary of the Navy of the importance of such an undertaking, he corresponded with leading scientists in other nations, asking them to promote such a project.[15] The abstract logs collected by Maury as part of his system for gathering data for his wind and current charts are among the records of the Weather Bureau. Among them are letters from Captain William H. Smyley, U.S. sealer who was for a half century the source for the lowest temperature recorded in Antarctica.[16] The abstract log, October 13-December 22, 1853, kept by Captain John J. Heard of Boston on the commercial voyage from Boston to Melbourne in the bark *Oriental*, during which he discovered Heard Island, was published by Maury.[17]

Congressional documents of the House of Representatives and of the Senate during the 1830's contain many letters and testimonials from citizens who were interested in a national exploring expedition. Among these are many letters from Captain Fanning.[18] Also included is the report prepared for the Secretary of the Navy by Jere-

ment of State, NA. See also James Byers to Daniel Parker, August 17 and 25, and September 4, 1820, in Miscellaneous Letters, August-October, 1820, RG 59, NA.

[15] Herman R. Friis, "Matthew Fontaine Maury, Captain, U.S. Navy," *Bulletin of the United States Antarctic Projects Officer*, I (February, 1960), 23-29. *See also* Letters Received, March, 1840-January, 1885, and Letters Sent ("Letter Book," "Record," or "Records"), July, 1842-November, 1862, RG 78, Records of the Naval Observatory, NA.

[16] Abstract Log Collection of Matthew Fontaine Maury, RG 27, Records of the Weather Bureau, NA. See also Index to Abstract Logs Received Between 1853 and 1861, RG 78, NA; and Letters Received Relating to Hydrography, 1842-62, RG 45, NA. For a printed version of Smyley's remarks see Maury, *Explanations and Sailing Directions to Accompany the Wind and Current Charts* (hereafter cited as *Explanations and Sailing Directions*) (5th ed.; Washington, 1853), pp. 407-413.

[17] Maury, *Explanations and Sailing Directions* (7th ed.; Philadelphia, 1855), pp. 763-768. The logbook of the *Oriental* kept during the voyage and the diary of Mrs. Fidelia Reed Heard, who accompanied her husband on the voyage, are the property of David B. Heard, a great-grandson, Waban, Mass.

[18] See, for instance, Fanning's "Memorial" of December 18, 1833, published as S. Doc. 10, 23 Cong., 1 sess., Serial 238.

miah N. Reynolds (see footnote 13) from interviews with New England sealers and whalers and from examinations of their records as a prelude to the proposed naval expedition of 1828-29.[19]

III. SCIENTIFIC EXPLORATION AND RESEARCH

A. The United States Exploring Expedition, 1838-42

The United States Exploring Expedition of 1838-42, commonly called the Wilkes Expedition after its commander, Lieutenant Charles Wilkes, was the first scientific exploring expedition sent to the Antarctic by the U.S. Government. Although it was primarily concerned with exploring the Pacific Basin, three cruises were made into the Antarctic—two in February, 1839, and one in January and February, 1840. The 1839 cruises south from the coast of Tierra del Fuego were too late in the season to accomplish much more than give the men experience, although the *Flying Fish* maneuvered through the pack ice to 70° S., 101°16′ W., about 110 miles north of Thurston Island. The cruise of the *Vincennes* and the *Porpoise* in 1840 along the edge of the pack ice fringing the continent from 160° E. to 100° E., a distance of approximately 1,500 nautical miles, ranks as one of the great feats of antarctic exploration.

There is a considerable amount of published and manuscript material pertaining to the various facets of the Wilkes Expedition. An indispensable tool to guide the researcher through this labyrinth was written by Daniel C. Haskell.[20]

1. PUBLISHED WORKS

Only a small part of the official reports pertain to Antarctica.[21] This reflects the relatively short time that the expedition spent in the far south and the fact that none of the nine members of the civilian

[19] Reynolds' report was published as H. Doc. 105, 23 Cong., 2 sess., Serial 273; and, somewhat revised, as part of S. Doc. 262, 24 Cong., 1 sess., Serial 281, pp. 55-87.

[20] Daniel C. Haskell, *The United States Exploring Expedition, 1838-1842, and Its Publications, 1844-1874* (hereafter cited as *Exploring Expedition*) (New York, 1942).

[21] Charles Wilkes *et al.*, *United States Exploring Expedition During the Years 1838, 1839, 1840, 1841, 1842* (hereafter cited as *U.S. Exploring Expedition*) (22 quarto vols. and 12 atlases; Philadelphia, 1844-74).

scientific corps accompanied the vessels on the 1840 cruise. The antarctic cruises were well covered by Wilkes in his *Narrative*.[22] The meteorological data were incorporated into a volume of the official reports,[23] and part of them were included in brief tables in the *Narrative*.[24] The data on terrestrial magnetism, which was to have been prepared for publication by Wilkes, has been used by others;[25] however, Wilkes' "Chart of the Antarctic Continent" carries isogonic lines.[26]

The published works range in subject matter from the prolonged and controversial preparation of the expedition to arguments as to what Wilkes did or did not see in 1840 off what is now known as Oates Coast.[27] It is beyond the scope of this paper to even summarize the publications of and about the Wilkes Expedition. This has been done well by Haskell and by several participants in the symposium organized by the American Philosophical Society in 1940 to

[22] Charles Wilkes, *Narrative of the United States Exploring Expedition During the Years 1838, 1839, 1840, 1841, 1842* (hereafter cited as *Narrative*) (5 vols. and 1 atlas; Philadelphia, 1845). For the antarctic cruises, see I, 131-161, 394-400, and 405-414; and II, 279-365 and 453-473. For a discussion of the various issues of the *Narrative*, see Haskell, *Exploring Expedition*, pp. 31-47.

[23] Wilkes, *Meteorology*, Vol. XI of *U.S. Exploring Expedition* (Philadelphia, 1851).

[24] Wilkes, *Narrative*, II (Philadelphia, 1845), 459, 460, 464.

[25] C. C. Ennis, "Magnetic Results of the United States Exploring Expedition, 1838-1842," *Terrestrial Magnetism and Atmospheric Electricity*, XXXIX, No. 2 (1934), 91-100; G. W. Littlehales, "The South Magnetic Pole," *Bulletin of the American Geographical Society*, XLII (January, 1910), 1-8; and F. W. Reichelderfer, "The Contributions of Wilkes to Terrestrial Magnetism, Gravity and Meteorology," *Centenary Celebration, The Wilkes Exploring Expedition of the United States Navy, 1838-1842, and Symposium on American Polar Exploration, February 23-24, 1940* (hereafter cited as *Centenary Celebration*), *Proceedings of the American Philosophical Society*, LXXXII (Philadelphia, June, 1940), 583-600.

[26] Wilkes, "Chart of the Antarctic Continent, Shewing [*sic*] the Icy Barrier Attached to it. Discovered by the U.S. Ex-Ex., Charles Wilkes, Esq., Commander, 1840," printed as the second map in *Atlas, Narrative*. It was also printed as the second map in *Atlas of Charts*, Vol. I of 2 vols. accompanying Wilkes, *Hydrography, U.S. Exploring Expedition*, XXIII (Philadelphia, 1861).

[27] The controversies relating to the organization, the scientific corps, and the publication of the official reports of the expedition are dealt with by Harley Harris Bartlett, "The Reports of the Wilkes Expedition, and the Work of the Specialists in Science," *Centenary Celebration, Proceedings of the American Philosophical Society*, LXXXII (Philadelphia, June, 1940), 601-705. For a well-documented account of the expedition from its inception to its conclusion, see Philip I. Mitterling, *America in the Antarctic to 1840* (Urbana, Ill., 1959), pp. 67-168.

mark the centennial of the expedition.[28]

Wilkes' "Chart of the Antarctic Continent," showing the edge of the pack ice as he encountered it from 167° E. to 97° E., was the major contribution of the expedition as far as Antarctica is concerned. Land had been sighted from the *Peacock* before it was forced to retreat in damaged condition and from the *Porpoise* and *Vincennes* at various points along this 1,500-mile stretch. Wilkes exercised a high degree of cartographic integrity. He distinguished clearly between what he called the "icy barrier" and land, and he showed the latter only where it had been sighted and not as a continuous coastline. However, on the basis of sighting land at so many places, he concluded that they were indeed parts of a continent.[29]

Wilkes' concept of an Antarctic Continent was rejected by many, including no less a personality than Sir James Clark Ross, leader of the British Antarctic Expedition, 1839-43. We cannot discuss here this controversy and the authenticity of Wilkes' landfalls. This has been done elsewhere.[30] It will suffice to invite you to compare the close approximation in both configuration and geographical position of Wilkes' landfalls and the coastal configuration on a modern map of that part of Antarctica.

2. MANUSCRIPT MATERIAL

There is a vast collection of manuscript material relating to the Wilkes Expedition, only a small part of which relates to Antarctica. Most of it is in the National Archives, including the correspondence

[28] Haskell, *Exploring Expedition;* and *Centenary Celebration, Proceedings of the American Philosophical Society,* LXXXII (Philadelphia, June, 1940), 519-705.

[29] Wilkes, *Narrative,* II, 334-335.

[30] Kenneth J. Bertrand, "Wilkes' Antarctic Discoveries Now Fully Confirmed," *Bulletin of the United States Antarctic Projects Officer,* I (February, 1960), 19-22; William Herbert Hobbs, "Wilkes Land Rediscovered," *The Geographical Review,* XXII (October, 1932), 632-655; W. H. Hobbs, "The Discovery of Wilkes Land, Antarctica," *Centenary Celebration, Proceedings of the American Philosophical Society,* LXXXII (Philadelphia, June, 1940), 561-582; B. P. Lambert and P. G. Law, "A New Map of the Coastline of Oates Land and Eastern King George V Land," (typescript) delivered November 18, 1959, at the Antarctic Symposium, Buenos Aires; Douglas Mawson, "Wilkes' Antarctic Landfalls," *Proceedings of the Royal Geographical Society of Australasia,* South Australian Branch, XXXIV, sess. 1932-33 (1934), 70-113; and James Clark Ross, *A Voyage of Discovery and Research in the Southern and Antarctic Regions During the Years 1839-43,* I (London, 1847), pp. 273-276, 285-299, 346-359.

between the Secretary of the Navy and various individuals from the President of the United States to civilian scientists seeking a place on the expedition.[31] The correspondence of Wilkes includes his reports to the Secretary of the Navy and the letters sent by the Secretary of the Navy throughout the expedition.[32] Wilkes' detractors accused him of making false claims relating to his first landfalls in Antarctica in 1840; and part of the testimony in the proceedings of his court-martial, following the close of the expedition,[33] pertains to circumstances during the occasions when land was sighted. Helpful in understanding the atmosphere in which the official reports of the expedition were prepared and published is Wilkes' correspondence with publishers and Members of Congress during the decades following the expedition.[34]

Each civilian scientist and naval officer was required to keep a journal during the expedition. Many of these journals and the logbooks of the ships are in the National Archives and are of major importance.[35] However, in spite of the order that all journals, notes, memoranda, sketches, and natural history specimens were to be surrendered to the commanding officer of each ship to be placed at the disposal of the Navy Department, many of them today are lost or are the property of libraries and museums scattered over the country. Haskell devotes 147 entries to manuscript material relating to the expedition located in 21 different repositories, only one of which is the National Archives.[36]

[31] Miscellaneous Letters Sent ("General Letter Book") by the Secretary of the Navy, June, 1798-November, 1886, RG 45, NA.

[32] Letters From Officers Commanding Expeditions, January, 1818-December, 1885, RG 45, NA.

[33] Proceedings of General Courts Martial, Courts of Inquiry, Boards of Investigation, and Boards of Inquest, RG 125, Records of the Office of the Judge Advocate General (Navy), Washington National Records Center, Suitland, Md.

[34] See, for instance, Wilkes' "Petition" of February, 1849, 30A-H11.1, in Petitions and Memorials, RG 46, Records of the United States Senate, NA; his "Memorial" of February, 1857, 34A-H10, in Petitions and Memorials, RG 46, NA; and his "Memorial" of January, 1876, Sen. 44A-D1, report 60, in Committee Reports, RG 46, NA.

[35] For journals kept by the officers on the antarctic cruises, see Journals and Logs Kept by Members of the Wilkes Expedition, 1838-42, RG 37, Records of the Hydrographic Office, NA. For logbooks of the ships, see Logs of United States Naval Ships and Stations, 1801-1946, RG 24, Records of the Bureau of Naval Personnel, NA.

[36] Haskell, *Exploring Expedition,* pp. 129-139.

B. Twentieth-Century Expeditions

1. PUBLISHED WORKS

The research worker concerned with twentieth-century U.S. antarctic expeditions is confronted with problems that differ only in degree from those related to the Wilkes Expedition source material. Publications are many and varied, journals and manuscripts are scattered, and there is an unknown quantity of fugitive material.

Five books, including Rear Admiral Richard E. Byrd's own narrative, three monographs, and 18 articles resulted from the first Byrd expedition to Antarctica, 1928-30.[37] Four books, including two by Byrd, four monographs, and 33 articles were produced by members of Byrd's second expedition to Antarctica, 1933-35, and their associates.[38] In the absence of published, official scientific reports, foreigners have sometimes questioned the scientific objectives of the Byrd expeditions. However, the above tally indicates a rather considerable output. Owing to the fact that the articles have appeared in a wide variety of professional journals, even antarctic specialists are generally unaware of the amount that has been published. The *Antarctic Bibliography* has done much to correct this oversight.[39]

[37] The books and monographs include: Harry Adams, *Beyond the Barrier With Byrd* (Chicago, 1932); Richard E. Byrd, *Little America* (New York, 1930); Laurence McKinley Gould, *Cold* (New York, 1931); W. L. G. Joerg, *The Work of the Byrd Antarctic Expedition, 1928-1930* (New York, 1930); J. S. O'Brien, *By Dog Sled for Byrd* (Chicago, 1931); and Paul Siple, *A Boy Scout With Byrd* (New York, 1931). See also the items in footnote 38 by G. Grimminger and W. C. Haines.

[38] The books and monographs include: Byrd, *Alone* (New York, 1938); Byrd, *Discovery* (New York, 1935); G. Grimminger, "Meteorological Results of the Byrd Antarctic Expeditions, 1928-30, 1933-35: Summaries of Data," *Monthly Weather Review*, Supplement 42 (February, 1941); G. Grimminger and W. C. Haines, "Meteorological Results of the Byrd Antarctic Expeditions, 1928-30, 1933-35: Tables," *Monthly Weather Review*, Supplement 41 (October, 1939); Joe Hill, Jr., and Ola Davis Hill, *In Little America With Byrd* (Boston, 1937); Thomas C. Poulter, *Geophysical Studies in the Antarctic* (Stanford, n. d.); T. C. Poulter, *Meteor Observations in the Antarctic, Byrd Antarctic Expedition II, 1933-1935*, Pt. 1 (Stanford, 1955); and Paul A. Siple, *Scout to Explorer* (New York, 1936). Of monographic quality and scope is a series of papers by Gladys E. Baker, Edwin B. Bartram, Carroll W. Dodge, and Paul A. Siple under the general heading of "The Second Byrd Antarctic Expedition—Botany," *Annals of the Missouri Botanical Garden*, XXV (April, 1938), 467-727.

[39] U.S. Naval Photographic Interpretation Center [John H. Roscoe, comp.], *Antarctic Bibliography* (Washington, 1951).

Some may question the propriety of considering the two antarctic expeditions of Sir Hubert Wilkins as U.S. undertakings. Sir
Hubert was not a U.S. citizen, but he spent many years in this country. He used U.S. equipment, his expeditions were carried out under
the auspices of the American Geographical Society, and his principal
financial backers were Americans.

Sir Hubert was also associated with Lincoln Ellsworth in the
latter's four visits to Antarctica. Both the Wilkins and the Ellsworth
expeditions were essentially aeronautical, with scientific investigation limited to meteorological observation. However, because of
their effect on the interpretation of the geography of the Antarctic
Peninsula and because of Ellsworth's epic transantarctic flight in
1935, a number of publications have resulted. Ellsworth himself
wrote one book[40] and five articles, and Wilkins wrote two articles.
Five other articles relating to Ellsworth's expeditions and one relating to Wilkins' expeditions have been published.

The United States Antarctic Service (USAS) Expedition, 1939-
41, was cut short by World War II, and expedition members became
involved in military service as soon as they reached home. As a result,
the opportunity for preparation of scientific results was limited and
delayed. For some expedition personnel, involvement in other activities following the war precluded further work on expedition matters.
Two volumes directly resulted from the expedition. The first was
prepared by then Commander Robert A. J. English, who had been
Executive Secretary to the Executive Committee of the expedition.[41]
The second was a collection of 40 reports of varying length by members of the expedition and others issued by the American Philosophical Society.[42] At least 12 other articles and one monograph dealing
with results of the expedition have been published.

Following World War II there were three U.S. expeditions to
Antarctica before activities for IGY began. They included the first
and second U.S. Navy Developments Projects, commonly referred to
as *Operation Highjump* (1946-47) and *Operation Windmill* (1947-

---

[40] Lincoln Ellsworth, *Beyond Horizons* (New York, 1937).

[41] *Sailing Directions for Antarctica,* Hydrographic Office Pub. 138 (Washington,
1943).

[42] *Reports on Scientific Results of the United States Antarctic Service Expedition,
1939-1941, Proceedings of the American Philosophical Society,* LXXXIX (Philadelphia,
April, 1945).

48). The primary objectives of *Highjump* were to obtain aerial photographs of a large part of the margins of Antarctica and to test and adapt standard military equipment for the purposes of polar exploration. The objective of *Windmill* was to obtain ground control for the *Highjump* photography. In spite of these limited objectives, two books and parts of three others have resulted from *Highjump*, and four monographs and seven articles have been based on the activities of either or both operations.[43]

The third U.S. expedition to the far south after World War II was the Ronne Antarctic Research Expedition, 1946-48, the last privately organized antarctic expedition. Judged by present standards, Ronne's expedition was a small one, but much valuable work was accomplished. Thirteen technical reports of varying length were published. Ronne's narrative was published as a book,[44] and he also wrote four journal articles. At least two other articles and one book were written by other members of the expedition.

2. NEWSPAPER ACCOUNTS

Newspapers have provided important information concerning early sealers, and they are no less important as a source for information about modern exploring expeditions. The organizations, preparations, departures, and arrivals of modern expeditions have been covered by metropolitan dailies, and all modern expeditions have sold newspaper rights or have been accompanied by reporters from newspapers and wire services. Consequently, many details omitted from popular narratives of expeditions can be obtained from newspaper accounts. For this the files of the *New York Times*, available on microfilm in many libraries, are especially valuable. Special

[43] Some of these are: Henry C. Bailey, "Electronics in the Antarctic," *Electronics*, XX (August, 1947), 82-88; Robert S. Dietz, "Some Oceanographic Observations on Operation HIGHJUMP: Final Report," *Report*, No. 55 (U.S. Navy Electronics Laboratory, 1948); Thomas R. Henry, *The White Continent, The Story of Antarctica* (New York, 1950); William H. Kearns, Jr., and Beverley Britton, *The Silent Continent* (New York, 1955), pp. 162-203; William J. Menster, *Strong Men South* (Milwaukee, 1949); [John Roscoe], *Regional Photo Interpretation Series: Antarctica*, U.S. Air Force Manual 200-30 (Washington, August, 1953); Walter Sullivan, *Quest for a Continent* (New York, 1957), pp. 173-261; Charles W. Thomas, *Ice Is Where You Find It* (Indianapolis, 1951); and U.S. War Department, *Army Observers' Report of Operation Highjump, Task Force 68, U.S. Navy* (Washington, 1947).

[44] Finn Ronne, *Antarctic Conquest* (New York, 1949).

commendation must be given to August Howard for his dedicated work in publishing the *Polar Times*. His careful collection of excerpts from the *New York Times* and other sources has been an invaluable aid to the polar historian.

3. MANUSCRIPT MATERIAL

A considerable amount of manuscript material relating to modern scientific exploration in Antarctica has already been accumulated. In addition to the material in the National Archives relating to Rear Admiral Richard E. Byrd, a large body of his personal papers is in possession of his heirs in Boston. As of this date it has not been made available to scholars. Pictures and notes of Sir Hubert Wilkins are on file in the American Geographical Society, and the society also has a composite log of Ellsworth's transantarctic flight of 1935 compiled by William Briesemeister from Ellsworth's journal, Hollick-Kenyon's log, and radio messages received by the *Wyatt Earp* from the plane. There are also typescripts of Ellsworth's diary, Hollick-Kenyon's log, and the sheets on which Ellsworth's navigation was recalculated for the purposes of determining map positions.

The largest collection of manuscript material relating to modern U.S. antarctic expeditions is in the National Archives. First, in order of time, are thousands of feet of moving pictures and still photographs taken on the first and second Byrd expeditions.[45] Here also are the papers of Captain Harold E. Saunders,[46] close personal friend of Byrd and cartographer for these expeditions. The maps of the Byrd expeditions are based on Saunders' calculations and his pioneering methods for plotting positions of relief features from aerial photographs. Saunders was also chairman of the Advisory Committee on Antarctic Names of the U.S. Board on Geographic Names for two decades. His correspondence with Byrd and his notes on his efforts to reconcile the features on earlier maps with features shown in Byrd photographs are basic to the history of geographical nomenclature in Byrd Land.

[45] The motion picture film is in RG 200, Gift Motion Pictures in the National Archives, NA; the still pictures are in the *New York Times* (Paris Office) files, RG 306, Records of the United States Information Agency, NA.

[46] Saunders' papers are in RG 401, Private Papers on Polar Regions Given to the National Archives, NA.

The notebooks, papers, and correspondence of Paul A. Siple, whose antarctic connection extends from the first Byrd expedition to the first winter at the South Pole during IGY, and of Carl R. Eklund, a member of the USAS Expedition and leader of the U.S. Wilkes Station during IGY, are in the custody of the Center for Polar Archives.[47]

In view of the fact that World War II interfered with the planned publication of the scientific results of the USAS Expedition, it is fortunate that many of the records are now located in the National Archives. They consist of a wide variety of material relating to the inception, organization, operation, and conclusion of the expedition. They include official orders, directives, and minutes; correspondence; field notes, journals, and operational orders; and a vast amount of film of all kinds. Most of the records are from the Division of Territories and Island Possessions of the Department of the Interior, but related material is included in the records of the Office of the Secretary of the Navy, the Chief of Naval Operations, the Hydrographic Office, and the United States Coast Guard.[48]

Three originally classified, mimeographed volumes prepared for limited official distribution contain most of the history of *Highjump*,[49] and a comparable single volume relates to *Windmill.*[50]

IV. THE VALUE OF TWENTIETH-CENTURY MANUSCRIPT RECORDS

One might well ask, of what value are these manuscript records of the twentieth-century scientific exploring expeditions? Narrative volumes written by Byrd, Gould, Siple, Ellsworth, and Ronne have been published and a variety of articles have appeared in professional scientific journals. What more of significance can be added in view of the extensive program of surveying and scientific investigation that has been carried on continuously since 1956? Equipment is more

[47] Siple's and Eklund's papers are in RG 401, NA.

[48] For a guide to this material, *see* National Archives, *Records of the United States Antarctic Service,* Preliminary Inventory No. 90 (Washington, 1955).

[49] Commander, Task Force 68, *Report on Antarctic Developments Project, 1947 (Operation Highjump)* [1947], CTF68/A9/rdk, Serial 0184.

[50] Commander, Task Force 39, *Report of Operations, Second Antarctic Development[s] Project, 1947-1948* [1948], CTF39/A9/rdk, Serial 045.

efficient, instrumentation is more sophisticated, and technological advance has placed logistics on a plane that was undreamed of in 1928.

The answer to the question regarding the value of these records is threefold. A definitive history of U.S. antarctic exploration has not been written. Perhaps this will never be possible for the discoveries of the early sealers. The body of records now brought together here, however, is the raw material for such an undertaking for the twentieth-century exploring expeditions. Before a definitive history can be written for any part of the modern era, however, a great deal of fugitive material must be located and made available. Today we are opening a center where this can be collected and maintained.

Perhaps almost as important as a definitive history of U.S. activity in Antarctica, and certainly more attainable, is a narrative related to the scientific achievement. Understandably, narratives by leaders of private expeditions are designed partly to pay expenses, and they must have a broad popular appeal. For this reason discovery, adventure, and danger rather than scientific investigation have been emphasized in most narratives. Actually, there is more tedium than glamour involved in most modern scientific investigation, but that does not diminish its importance. Often it is the scientist at home analyzing the data who generally experiences the thrill of discovery and not the man at the lonely antarctic base who made the routine instrumental observations. Until a narrative involving the scientific activity of the U.S. expeditions has been written, the really important scientific achievements of our twentieth-century explorers will remain insufficiently known.

Since 1928 we have been accumulating an increasing volume of better and better aerial photographs of Antarctica. Earlier photographic flight lines in many cases can be placed on the map only approximately from the navigator's flight log. If it is important for historical reasons to do so, the exact line of these flights probably can now be determined by correlating the earlier photographs with later ones that have been identified in terms of known features on the latest topographic maps.

The record of time is not the exclusive property of the historian. Time is also an important element in the natural sciences. Only through records of former observations can changes in natural phenomena be detected. The longer the record of instrumental observation, the more valuable are the data in meteorology, earth magnetism, tides, aurora, and seismology. Earlier photographs can be compared with later ones of the same area for evidence of changes in sea ice, the retreat or advance of glacier ice, and the extent of seasonal snow cover in ice-free areas.

It is obvious that the records deposited at the National Archives are of value to both the historian and the scientist concerned with current problems in the natural sciences. The more complete these records are, the greater their value.

COMMENTS ON LEGISLATION
FOR A RICHARD E. BYRD
ANTARCTIC COMMISSION

James E. Mooney

A close friend and associate of Rear Admiral Richard E. Byrd, Dr. Mooney has played a large role in planning and coordinating U.S. antarctic programs among Government agencies, private institutions, and individuals. He was Deputy U.S. Antarctic Projects Officer, 1959-64. In 1964 he was appointed Special Assistant to the Assistant Secretary of Defense. He retired on December 31, 1965. [Dr. Mooney died on October 27, 1968.]

I am proud to have a part in these discussions and am cognizant of the responsibility the National Archives is assuming by instituting the Center for Polar Archives in which to preserve important papers relating to U.S. interests and activities in polar regions. The United States has a glorious past in polar exploration; its present is vigorous and stimulating. The records of all past and present activity should be preserved for use in planning future activities as well as in compiling an authentic and definitive history.

Time and again I have stated the need for a comprehensive history of the accomplishments and activities of all U.S. polar expeditions. We need one, also, for the splendid operational and logistical support supplied by the Armed Forces since the end of World War II. I do not mean to imply that organized data and material are unavailable for the writing of these histories. But much that is available is widely scattered, thereby presenting difficulties to the historian. The Center for Polar Archives will hopefully alleviate this problem for the historian, at least as far as current and future records are concerned.

Kenneth J. Bertrand, in his paper, has offered a running ac-

count of historical research sources. His scholarly paper represents years of researching and sifting through records in libraries, archives, and private collections. He has formulated a basis on which to tell the great events; he has provided guidance for finding the facts; and he has hinted at the satisfaction that one can have in finding them. He has opened the diary of the United States in Antarctica.

Both Paul A. Siple and Rear Admiral Richard B. Black have presented papers covering one chapter of the diary—the chapter dealing with the modern beginnings of our Government's increasingly active part in the exploration of Antarctica and the attempts to discover the secrets of this ice-locked continent. Siple's approach has been that of organization and planning; Black's approach has been that of the field explorer. Many of the facts they have enunciated are preserved in the records of the United States Antarctic Service Expedition here in the National Archives.

Another, more recent, chapter of the diary has been the effort to formulate within our Government's executive branch an administrative unit for antarctic programs. At the request of a number of Congressmen, I have been largely responsible for preparing the content of bills proposing the establishment of such a unit to be known as the Richard E. Byrd Antarctic Commission. These bills have been introduced at each session of the House of Representatives from the Eighty-sixth Congress to the present one (Ninetieth). Many Congressmen have felt that our Government's activity in antarctic programs should be brought together at a high level because many departments and agencies have increased their interest and involvement in antarctic research and logistics since just after World War II. Since the signing of the Antarctic Treaty in late 1959 with 11 other nations, it has been felt by some people to be even more important to centralize this country's antarctic activities and interests. The Richard E. Byrd Antarctic Commission has been envisioned as a means of developing, administering, and implementing U.S. antarctic programs in the national interest while preventing duplication among Government agencies and private institutions.

I would like to outline briefly the concept of the proposed commission as contained in the bills mentioned above. For this outline I will refer to the bill introduced in the House on January 11, 1965, by Representative Craig Hosmer of California. This bill is representative of all the others.

The purpose of the proposed commission as stated in the bill would be:

> to provide for continuity and support of study, research, and development of programs for peaceful uses in science, commerce, and other activities related to Antarctica, which shall include, but shall not be limited to, gathering, evaluating, correlating, and dispersing of information and knowledge obtained from exploration, research, and other mediums relating to weather, communications, travel, and other areas of information; also to coordinate Antarctic activities among those agencies of the United States Government and private institutions interested in or concerned directly with the promotion, advancement, increase, and diffusion of knowledge of the Antarctic; and to direct and administer United States Antarctic programs in the national interest.[1]

Among its functions, the proposed commission would maintain a depository of information relating to Antarctica; conduct field and laboratory studies for the advancement of knowledge of Antarctica in science, commerce, and related activities; publish or provide for the publication of scientific, technical, historical, and general information about Antarctica; approve the plans for and supervise Antarctic activities conducted or supported by Federal agencies except those of a military nature; and make arrangements for the conduct of scientific research and other scholarly activities in Antarctica by private or public institutions or persons that would implement the purposes of the commission.

To administer the commission, there would be a director, two deputy directors, and a board of governors. The funding of the commission would be accomplished by the usual governmental procedure. The commission would be able to use the staff, services, facilities, and information of any U.S. agency on a reimbursable basis as long as the primary purposes of the agency were not interfered with. The U.S. Navy would provide the necessary logistical and operational support on a reimbursable basis.

The commission would prescribe criteria for the establishment of research centers at academic and research institutions having special facilities for or interests in scientific research in Antarctica.

---

[1] H. R. 2211, 89 Cong., 1 sess., 1965, p. 1.

The development and coordination of research programs at these centers would be the responsibility of the commission. The commission would be authorized to grant funds to permit qualified students and others to conduct studies pertinent to Antarctica.

The bills proposing the commission were referred to the House Committee on Interior and Insular Affairs, a subcommittee of which held hearings. I am sorry, as are hundreds of others, that none of the bills ever reached the House floor even though the subcommittee voted favorably and recommended enactment.

SESSION IV
Writing and Research
on the Arctic

CHAIRMAN:

Oliver W. Holmes

Dr. Holmes has been Executive Director of the National Historical Publications Commission, which encourages by support the publication of private papers of outstanding U.S. citizens, since 1961. He joined the National Archives staff in 1936. Before 1936 he taught history at Montana State University and held several editorial positions.

The fourth session contains papers written by three persons who well illustrate by their own experience and work the importance of consulting official records and private papers. The first paper presents the problems of a biographer when his source material is widely scattered; the second views the importance of the Arctic through the history of a Government organization established during World War II for the purpose of aiding the war effort by finding out more about nontemperate environments; and the third looks at polar exploration and research through the eyes of a scientist who has had much experience with fieldwork in polar regions. The papers will be followed by comments from the distinguished lady who has edited the Arctic Bibliography *since its inception.*

BIOGRAPHY AND THE PRESERVATION
OF PRIVATE PAPERS

Chauncey C. Loomis

Professor of English literature at Dartmouth College, Dr.
Loomis has a special interest in the history of exploration,
particularly exploration in the polar regions. He has made
three trips to the Arctic and sub-Arctic. During the last few
years he has done concentrated research for his biography
of Charles Francis Hall.

Several years ago when I started work on my biography of Charles
Francis Hall, I went to Cincinnati, Ohio, to see what I could
find about Hall's early life—the years before he first went to the
Arctic in 1860. Hall is an obscure, lonely, eccentric figure in the
history of arctic exploration. When he set out north for the first time,
ill-equipped and virtually alone, he was thirty-nine years old, a small-
time Cincinnati businessman who had been no farther north than
New Hampshire. (He prepared himself for arctic life by camping in
a pup tent on Cincinnati's Mount Adams—hardly fit preparation for
what he was to endure.) Hall believed that he had been called by
God and that he was destined to find survivors of the Franklin expedition. It was, of course, wishful thinking. Franklin's two ships, the
Erebus and the *Terror,* had disappeared into the Canadian Archipelago in 1845; by 1859, when Hall suddenly decided to leave his
family and his business to go north, more than twenty expeditions
had been sent out after Franklin and more than $4 million had been
spent in the search. Major geographical discoveries had been made,
but all that had been found of the Franklin expedition were some
pathetic relics, a few graves and skeletons, and one ominous cairn
message. By 1859 anyone with any sense had given up hope of sur-

vivors, but Hall believed that he could do alone what navies and governments had failed to do. Just as the curtain was coming down on the Franklin tragedy, he elbowed his way on stage—bearded and squat, only half-educated and rather vulgar after all the aristocrats, naval officers, statesmen, and tycoons who had been on stage before him.

It was the beginning of a remarkable career in exploration—a career that was at least partly documented once it began. But the first thirty-nine years of Hall's life were very obscure, and so I went to Cincinnati to see what I could find out about them.

Leafing through the Cincinnati telephone directory in my hotel room, I found among all the Halls listed the name Franklin Hall. Gambling on the odd chance, I called this Franklin Hall and asked him if he was a descendant of Charles Francis Hall. His voice was suspicious, but he allowed that he was Hall's grandson. I eagerly announced that I was writing a book about his grandfather. There was a long silence—then his voice, very suspicious, simply asked, "Why?"

I could not give a satisfactory answer to that question then, and I cannot give one now, except to say that Hall's is a very good story and, like all good stories, is somehow significant. He was a man of terrific energy, the sort of a man who is bound to generate a good story if he goes out after something, and Hall went out after things with a drive and willpower that were amazing even in nineteenth-century America.

He was a lone wolf on his first two expeditions. He had to be: in spite of his heroic efforts to raise money, the cash budget for his first voyage was $980—for his second only about twice that amount. Actually, his poverty was a disguised blessing. During his two years on Baffin Island and his five years in the areas of Repulse Bay, Igloolik, and King William Island, he was forced to live with Eskimos as an Eskimo. He made geographical and historical discoveries: he proved that Frobisher Bay was a bay and not a strait, and that it was indeed the site of Martin Frobisher's sixteenth-century explorations. He made maps and charts that are surprisingly accurate considering his lack of formal training in navigation and cartography. Although he found no Franklin survivors, he added much to our knowledge of what happened to the expedition. But above all, it was his day-by-day life with Eskimos that made his first two expeditions remarkable in their time. From Eskimos he learned to live off the Arctic as few had done before him; his familiarity with their way of life was unequaled until Vilhjalmur Stefansson went north some forty years later.

His third and last expedition was another matter. By 1870 he had achieved a moderate fame, and the U.S. Government put him in command of an expedition that was to try to reach the North Pole. Congress appropriated $50,000 for the effort; Hall was given a ship, a crew, and even a staff of scientists. As some of you know, the *Polaris* expedition was a fiasco and a scandal. The fault was not Hall's, however, for he died early in the expedition, possibly murdered, and was buried far north on the western shores of Greenland.

Hall's is a good story, made even better by detail. A biographer must have detail—not just as evidence for his generalizations, but also as flesh and blood on the bones of his narration. It is the source of biographical detail that concerns me today.

To return for a moment to Franklin Hall's question, "Why?" When I interviewed the man the next morning, I discovered why he had asked. He knew almost nothing about his grandfather, and he was not very interested in him. In fact, he was not interested in history or in the past, except possibly his own. He had forgotten any family stories about his grandfather that he might have heard as a child; he had kept no sort of memorabilia. The world is full of persons like Franklin Hall who are indifferent to the past, and they are a curse to a biographer. Old letters, journals, and photographs are only so much junk to them. They like nothing more than a good bonfire fed by all the trash in the attic. What they burn is not necessarily a priceless record of the past; it usually deserves to be where it is, in the attic. Nevertheless, it is worth preserving for the private pleasure and edification of their own descendants if nothing else. On rainy afternoons in attics, many a child has suddenly been made aware of the reality of the past—and, incidentally, of mortality—by finding his grandfather's love letters or his grandmother's hats. And then, just possibly, someone like me might come along and actually use the stuff in a book.

A biographer must depend in part on private papers, on personal trivia, for his facts and for his understanding of his subject. The date on an otherwise useless letter might fix someone in a certain place at a certain time; canceled checks or receipted bills can show something not only about a man's financial situation, but also about his tastes; a hasty note written in love or anger always reveals much that is concealed in carefully considered, formal letters. Most valuable, of course, are private journals. They contain facts in a narrative sequence and simultaneously manifest a man's mind and personality.

In part, a biographer of an individual arctic explorer will use the same material that is used by a historian of exploration in general or by the chronicler of a single expedition, and he will consult similar sources. I have found official documents here at the National Archives, at the Naval Observatory, at the Stefansson Collection in Dartmouth College, at the Scott Polar Research Institute, at the American Geographical Society, and so on. But unless a biographer is writing a highly specialized and limited study, official letters and documents will not be enough. If he wants to write about the whole man, not simply a specialized machine, he needs personal and private papers as well as official records, journals as well as logs. The information that he needs has no defined limits or boundaries. Everything is grist for his mill.

I have been singularly fortunate. In the Division of Naval History at the Smithsonian Institution is a large collection of Hall material, which the Government purchased from his widow soon after his death. I have done research elsewhere—in New York, Cincinnati, Boston, London, Copenhagen, and Cambridge. I have even hired some Eskimos and personally retraced some of Hall's routes in the Canadian Arctic. But most of my work has been done at the Smithsonian. Concentrated in one place is a mass of material, most of it still in its original wrappers dated 1875. There are calling cards and business advertisements, lecture posters and newspaper clippings, railroad tickets and receipted bills, legal documents and photographs —most important, there are hundreds of letters and thousands of pages of manuscript journals. Contained in this mass of material, waiting to be reconstructed from the clutter, is the story of Charles Francis Hall. The letters and journals not only contain a story, they also evoke a period of U.S. history and supply fresh facts about the Arctic in the mid-nineteenth century. Hall was not a scientist, but he was a close observer and a painstaking taker of notes. He did not have any formal training in anthropology, for example (anyway, anthropology was at best an ill-defined discipline at the time), so his observations of Eskimo life are haphazard. But they are spontaneous, honest, and vivid. His journals also give a fine, detailed picture of life aboard nineteenth-century northern whalers. One typical anecdote concerns a sailor who had four of his toes frostbit. The captain decided that amputation was necessary and brought him to his cabin for the operation. Hall followed them to observe. The sailor, with only whisky as an anesthetic, remained stolid while three of his toes were removed. The fourth toe resisted amputation. While the captain hacked away at it, the sailor finally broke and shouted, "Damn that toe to hell!" Hall was a very pious man, unfortunately to the point of being stiff-necked. He reeled back at the sailor's blasphemy. That night, after describing the event in his journal, he wrote, "Under the circumstances it was enough to make one's blood run cold so extraordinarily wicked was the speech." The story illustrates the value of journals. In a log, the incident would have been recorded baldly: "Amputated four toes of seaman Brown this p.m." In Hall's journal, however, the incident vividly shows the harshness of life aboard arctic whalers and simultaneously reveals Hall's uncompromising piety in the context of that harsh and often profane life. This is the way with journals and letters—they vitalize and dramatize bare facts. It is one thing to be told that Hall was impoverished; it is another to read an entry in his journal written while he was trying to raise money in New York: "Started down the Bowery—sold damaged old hat to make a raise of 37 cts." A journal can reveal as much by what it does not say as by what it does say. Hall tried to raise money for his second expedition during the middle of the Civil War; so intent was he on his own purposes, so strong was his single-mindedness (admirable or reprehensible) that he simply ignored the national conflict. In letters and journals written in 1863 and 1864, he mentions the Civil War only four times.

Without the Smithsonian collection, Hall's biography could not be written. The collection is the sort of thing biographers dream about but all too seldom find. Usually the material about a man that survives him is scattered about the country [fig. 1], much of it hidden away where it can never be found. The creation of the Center for Polar Archives should help to solve this problem in the field of polar history. I only hope that, along with official records, some private papers end up here.

This is partly the responsibility of you who are here today. Most of you have been deeply involved with polar activities in recent years, and some of you have probably kept personal journals and records.

FIGURE 1—This photograph was found in Omaha, Nebr., where Hall had no known associations. With Hall are the men who helped plan the ill-fated *Polaris* expedition. Left to right: James Lupton, T. H. Stanton, Charles Francis Hall, and William P. Clark.

You should seriously consider making this material available to such an archives as this. A biography might not be written about you, but fifty or a hundred years from now a historian of our antarctic program, for example, might well be able to use your material. He will, of course, have all sorts of official records available to him, but official records only present part of the truth—or, more accurately perhaps, one kind of truth. In those records he will find the budgets, the lists of equipment, the official correspondence, and, most important, the accounts of scientific investigation and experiment. But what sort of men were involved with the program, and what were their motives? What about the covert political infighting that is inevitably involved in getting a program off the ground? What were the individual reactions to living in an isolated scientific community? What did the persons in that community think of one another? What about their individual reactions to the Antarctic—not their scientific studies of its glaciers or geology, but their aesthetic and psychological response to the whole environment?

Today's polar activities are tomorrow's history. No matter what their intrinsic merits today, tomorrow they will be the object of historical curiosity and scrutiny. Official documents will record these activities impersonally, but activities are created and carried out by individual human beings. Unless the personal records of those human beings are preserved, the truth about our polar activities as it will be known fifty or a hundred years from now will be only a partial truth.

A BRIEF HISTORY OF THE ARCTIC, DESERT, AND TROPIC INFORMATION CENTER AND ITS ARCTIC RESEARCH ACTIVITIES

Paul H. Nesbitt

Professor of anthropology at the University of Alabama, Dr. Nesbitt was Chief of the Arctic, Desert, and Tropic Information Center from 1948 until early in 1967. During World War II he served in the Office of Strategic Services and in the Arctic, Desert, and Tropic Information Center. He has led 15 scientific expeditions to various parts of the world and has written many books and articles about anthropology, environmental research, and life-support science.

The existence of the Arctic, Desert, and Tropic Information Center (ADTIC) is a vivid reminder, not only of the scale of global war, but of the many and diverse problems that operations on a global scale present. For our Armed Forces to operate successfully on a global basis, we must be knowledgeable about the world's different environments in which our forces now operate or are likely to operate in the future as well as about the peculiar operational problems that varied hostile environments present. Major adjustments must be made in areas of climatic extremes—not only physical adjustments but also those involving deep changes in mental and social attitudes prompted by new places, new customs, and new people. The need for an ADTIC is obvious: to save lives, to maintain equipment, and to increase the operational efficiency of our Armed Forces.

ESTABLISHMENT OF ADTIC

At the beginning of World War II our knowledge of the nontemperate areas of the world was either woefully weak or completely lacking. When, following the attack on Pearl Harbor, our Armed Forces moved into the South Pacific, the Aleutians, Greenland, and Africa and began to face the problems involved in long-range transport, bombing missions, and fighter operations (with the attendant incidents of forced landings in hostile environments), the need for information about the impact of climatic extremes on equipment, daily living, combat operations, and emergency survival became especially urgent.

By June, 1942, discussions in Washington had reached the stage of action. A directive memorandum ordered the setting up of a testing and research organization under the Proving Ground Command to collect and coordinate data concerning the Arctic and to initiate an exploratory trip to Houlton Field, Maine, to investigate that base's suitability for a cold weather testing detachment of the Proving Ground.[1]

In support of the establishment of a testing and research organization to supply needed information in order to facilitate operations in the Arctic, the man who was later to become the director of ADTIC wrote:

> . . . We have been impressed by the apparent lack of information concerning the different phases of life in the arctic
> . . . Although there is considerable research concerning arctic problems, much of it is poorly coordinated and seldom does it reach the parties who are directly concerned. Research on problems of diet, clothing, shelter, and the like has either been greatly retarded or there has been unnecessary duplication by lack of coordinated effort.
> . . . In this office we are getting reports from arctic detachments, many of which indicate deficiencies in equipment, food, and shelter. Although this information is passed on to those who

---

[1] Directive memorandum, "Arctic Research and Information Center for the Army Air Forces," to Colonel Grandison Gardner, Commanding Officer, Army Air Forces Proving Ground Command, Eglin Field, Fla., June 17, 1942.

are concerned with supplying our detachments, we have no way of knowing that the deficiencies are being corrected. . . .

Reports from Army Air Forces personnel returning from flights in the arctic all indicate the inadequacy of existing maps. Each flyer will correct his own map, but no effort is being made to prepare a master map of all corrections for the use of all flyers following a particular route. We also find that Air Force personnel flying over the Arctic are not consistent in the carrying of supplies necessary in the event there is an emergency landing.[2]

Several significant details stand out in the above directive memorandum and letter. Only the Arctic is involved; attaching the Center to the Proving Ground Command indicates the early intention to have it take charge of testing as well as documentary research; and the eventual sphere of activity is already clearly outlined—maps, equipment, food, and survival in emergencies.

Various revisions of the directive memorandum were made between June and September, 1942. The final version, the full text of which follows, departed considerably from the original draft.

1. There will be organized and operated by the Commanding General, Army Air Forces Proving Ground Command, at Eglin Field, Florida, an Information Center for the purpose of collecting, recording, coordinating, and preparing for publication pertinent data bearing upon the specialized operating conditions encountered by the Army Air Forces in conducting operations in arctic, desert, and tropic areas.
2. Information will be gathered by the Center from all available sources, with special attention to the experiments, findings, and conclusions of the Army Air Forces Cold Weather Testing Detachment and the Army Air Forces activities at the Desert Training Center.
3. The Information Center will be concerned with all phases of Air Force activities in arctic, desert, and tropic areas. This will include in its general scope such items as the specialized operation of all Army Air Forces equipment, shelter, food, medicine, and clothing, and selection and care of personnel. Special attention will be given to developing the best procedures to be used in case of forced landings, and to emergency kits for the maintenance of personnel in case of forced landings.

[2] Major William S. Carlson, Plans Division, Air Staff, to Colonel Grandison Gardner, June 19, 1942.

4. The Information Center will make recommendations regarding tables of organization and especially tables of basic allowances, as well as recommending from time to time appropriate action to the Director of Military Requirements, based upon its researches, findings, and conclusions.
5. The Information Center will not perform tests of any nature, but will make recommendations regarding research to the proper agencies.
6. The Information Center will furnish available information requested by the divisions, directorates, and commands of the Army Air Forces. It will also collect all possible information on air operations under the unusual weather conditions of the arctic, desert, and tropics, and will prepare this information for publication and dissemination to the Service in appropriate forms, such as Technical Manuals, Technical Orders, and Training Manuals. The manuscripts for these publications will be submitted to the Director of Military Requirements (AFROM) for processing and publication. The Information Center will also undertake such special studies as may be directed by the Commanding General, Army Air Forces.
7. The Information Center will maintain close liaison with the Cold Weather Testing Detachment, and the Army Air Forces activities at the Desert Training Center, in regard to the exchange of information pertinent to their activities.[3]

In September, 1942, the Acting Chief of the Center wrote a memorandum containing plans that would enable the Center to swing into action immediately upon activation.[4] Accompanying the memorandum was a list of personnel needed for the Center and a list of projects and studies that should be undertaken immediately. Among the projects were the development of procedures for forced landings in all nontemperate climates, the development of emergency kits, geographical and climatological studies of air routes over the polar icecap, the development of ways to package and ship foods to environments of extreme weather conditions, studies of ways to main-

[3] Directive memorandum, "Organization of an Arctic, Desert, Tropic Information Center," from Major General Muir S. Fairchild, Director, Military Requirements, to Brigadier General Grandison Gardner, Commanding General, Army Air Forces Proving Ground Command, September 20, 1942.
[4] Memorandum, "Present Status and Immediate Plans for the Arctic, Desert, Tropic Information Center," from Major Herbert O. Russell to Brigadier General Grandison Gardner, September, 1942.

tain health and morale in environments of climatic extremes, the development of clothing for flying and ground crews, and the revision of the tables of basic allowances for units in areas of environmental extremes.

The injunction against the performance of tests (paragraph 5 of the final directive memorandum in September, 1942), in effect removed the reason for the Center's attachment to the Proving Ground Command. Despite the hospitality of Eglin Field and the usefulness of the Technical Library attached to the Proof Department of the Command, it shortly became apparent that the location of the Center at Eglin was a handicap. Trips to Washington, New York, and other locations to gather information became increasingly necessary as the activities of the Center expanded. The Arctic Section, to perform at all adequately, required a northern base of operations. These factors brought about the removal of ADTIC from the Proving Ground Command in Florida to Headquarters, Army Air Force Office of Assistant Chief of Air Staff, Intelligence, New York City, in October, 1943. In April, 1944, the Center was transferred to Orlando Field, Florida, where it was attached to the Army Air Forces Tactical Center and redesignated the Arctic, Desert, and Tropic Branch of the AAF Tactical Center. Even after having been redesignated "Branch," it continued to operate under the 1942 directive memorandum until its deactivation in October, 1945.

At its peak ADTIC was staffed with about 80 military and civilian scientists, all experts in their special fields. These included biology; geography; geology; meteorology; physiology; psychology; and arctic, desert, and tropic operations. The scientists intermittently carried out studies in the arctic, desert, and tropic areas of the Americas, Africa, and Asia with the result that the general characteristics of these nontemperate environments became well known. From these studies more than 70 U.S. Air Force manuals, bulletins, and handbooks were published on subjects dealing with cold weather operations, survival, regional geography, operation and care of equipment, ethnology, biology, and botany. These publications were written by information specialists who had the unusual qualifications of thorough formal education coupled with long years of experience in arctic, desert, and tropic regions. When there arose a need for information on arctic areas that were then practically unknown, some of the staff took to the field. Scientists from the Center were on the

Greenland icecap from 1942 to 1944 securing new and important data on weather, permafrost, and operational requirements. The Center produced three training films on survival. These films, *Land and Live in the Arctic, Land and Live in the Jungle,* and *Land and Live in the Desert,* did more to educate airmen on the technique of emergency survival than any other single method of instruction. The high percentage of men who survived crash landings and bailouts in desert wastelands, jungles, and snow- and ice-covered areas is to a great extent due to these films and the survival information distributed by the Center.

Many of the foremost names in the history of polar research and exploration were staff members of the Center or associated with it through contracts. Among the prominent figures were Laurence M. Gould, Chief of the Arctic Branch, the work of which was by far the most important activity of the Center; Vilhjalmur Stefansson; Walter A. Wood; Richard F. Flint; A. Lincoln Washburn; Herbert G. Dorsey, Jr.; Alton Wade; John W. Marr; Paul Emile Victor; and Carl R. Eklund.

Among the significant accomplishments of the Center related to the Arctic were the following:

1. A comprehensive technical study of conditions that affect human health in the Arctic[5] and a bulletin on how to live in the Arctic.[6]

2. The preparation and publication of a topographic map of the Northern Hemisphere north of 39°30′ N. This was probably one of the most important single undertakings of the Center. The map was compiled on a polar stereographic projection and on a scale of 1:6,336,000 at 65° N. Coverage included relief by contour lines and hypsometric tints, transport facilities, graduated populated places, installations of a special type, and about 6,000 place names. The map, roughly 7 by 8 feet in size, was available both as a unit and as two separate sheets, one of North America and the other of Eurasia. Its contents were compiled from more than 2,500 different cartographic sources.

Accompanying the map was a publication that contained a cri-

[5] Arctic, Desert, and Tropic Information Center, *Medical Conditions in Arctic Regions,* Medical Series No. 1 (New York, 1944).

[6] Arctic, Desert, and Tropic Information Center, *Care of Personnel in the Arctic,* Informational Bulletin 8 (New York, 1944).

tique and evaluation of source materials used in compiling the map, a cartobibliography to the sources, and a detailed gazetteer of geographic names on the map.[7] For about ten years after publication it continued to be the most accurate and useful strategic planning chart of the Northern Hemisphere.

3. Environmental, life support, and operational studies pertaining to the Arctic. Chief among the technical reports and manuals were the following:

a. A comprehensive manual of operational procedures, apart from combat tactics, that have a bearing on the successful operation of aircraft under the peculiar conditions encountered in the Arctic.[8]

b. Manuals about the care of electronic equipment[9] and of aircraft in arctic areas.[10]

c. An area study of Alaska with particular reference to the solution of operational problems.[11]

d. A study describing the correct procedures, methods, and techniques of emergency survival in cold environments.[12]

REACTIVATION OF ADTIC

The reactivation of the Center in 1947 was prompted by the need for more recent, detailed, and specialized information on geography, climate, soil, transportation, and peoples of the nontemperate areas of the world. The information collected during World War II, although excellent, proved inadequate when measured in terms of

[7] U.S. Board on Geographical Names and the Arctic, Desert, and Tropic Branch of the AAF Tactical Center, *Gazetteer and List of Sources to Accompany (SP-5) Map of the Northern Hemisphere North of 39°30′ Showing Topography* (Washington, 1945).

[8] Arctic, Desert, and Tropic Information Center, *Aircraft Operations in the Arctic,* Informational Bulletin No. 12 (New York, 1944).

[9] Arctic, Desert, and Tropic Information Center, *Maintenance of Electronic Equipment in Non-Temperate Areas,* Informational Bulletin No. 17 (New York, 1944).

[10] Arctic, Desert, and Tropic Information Center, *Arctic Maintenance of Aircraft,* Informational Bulletin No. 15 (New York, 1944).

[11] Arctic, Desert, and Tropic Branch of the AAF Tactical Center, *Handbook of Alaska,* Informational Bulletin No. 18 (New York, 1945).

[12] Arctic, Desert, and Tropic Information Center, *Emergency Living in the Arctic,* Informational Bulletin No. 6 (New York, 1944).

contemporary military operational requirements. The Air University, Maxwell Air Force Base, Alabama, was delegated responsibility for maintaining the Center.

The mission of the Center, as stated by the organizing directive, is to collect, evaluate, and disseminate information bearing on Air Force operations in nontemperate areas.[13] It is primarily concerned with research in global geography, emphasizing areas of environmental extremes (the arctic, desert, and tropic areas) in which the Air Force operates and which are of strategic importance to the defense of the Western Hemisphere.

The research program is patterned on Air Force needs for geographical information and is conducted in two geographical fields: physical geography and cultural geography. The key objectives are to provide guidance in operational planning and implementation and to collect information directly applicable to the solutions of operational problems. Specific requirements come to the Center from the headquarters of the U.S. Air Force and major commands, including the Air Force Systems Command, the Strategic Air Command, the Tactical Air Command, and the U.S. Air Forces in Europe and the Pacific.

The research work of the organization is done by a staff of professional scientists, each of whom is a specialist in one or more scientific disciplines and combines extensive formal education with years of field experience. The disciplines represented are anthropology, botany, zoology, geography, and climatology. Information is collected through library and field research and liaison with research institutions and other scientists.

In 1964 the research emphasis of the Center shifted to the tropic and desert areas. Currently, the Center is not engaged in any major arctic project; the full activity of its staff is devoted to environmental research relating to Southeast Asia, equatorial Africa, and tropical America. However, the scope and character of arctic research done by the Center in the past is reflected in the following projects and activities:

1. *Project Mint Julep*—the investigation of smooth-ice areas of Greenland's icecap for use as landing strips.

This project was organized and put into the field in 1953. Exten-

[13] Directive from Commanding General, U.S. Air Force, to Commanding General, Air University, February 26, 1947.

sive scientific investigations were carried out for 4 months by a staff of 11 scientists in the fields of geology, glaciology, geography, and hydrography. They were loaned to the project by the American Geographical Society; the Snow, Ice, and Permafrost Research Establishment (SIPRE); the Engineer Research and Development Laboratories (ERDL); and the Arctic Construction and Frost Effects Laboratory (ACFEL). Transportation, the preparation of food, and complete maintenance service was provided by Northeast Air Command personnel from Sondre Stromfjord Air Base. The construction and administration of the camp were superbly supervised by John H. Nelles, formerly with ERDL and later with SIPRE.

The primary objective of the *Mint Julep* scientific program was to investigate the origin, extent, and permanence of the smooth-ice area first observed in 1947 during *Project Snowman* and the potentialities of the area as a natural landing strip for conventional aircraft. In addition, other information was sought, such as thermal profiles, melt-water runoff, permeability of the surface, weather forecasting, snow compaction, trafficability, and techniques of power drilling. Two technical reports covering the scientific results of the project were published by the Center.[14]

Mint Julep discovered that ridges between valleys are better sites for airstrips than frozen lakes. The ridges are basal glacial ice, strong enough to support landings by any aircraft now in operation. Further explorations demonstrated that near the *Mint Julep* campsite the exposed glacial ice extended in a belt about 10 miles wide at an altitude of 5,000 to 6,000 feet. Aerial observations and photographs suggested that this same belt extended along the fringe of the rough-ice area for hundreds of miles to the north and south along the west coast of Greenland. Many of these strips of exposed glacial ice could probably be used as landing fields in all seasons, while others would not be usable during the 4 to 6 weeks of summer weather.

The discovery of virtually ready-made landing strips for any size aircraft in an area with better weather and approach conditions than the Greenland coastal airbases offers a number of possibilities in many fields of air operations. Such landing areas are the logical bases from which to launch further explorations of the snow surface of the

[14] *Project Mint Julep*, Pt. I, ADTIC Publication A-104a, and Pt. II, ADTIC Publication A-104B (Maxwell Air Force Base, Ala., 1955).

icecap. Future weather observation stations, air rescue operations, and other support activities in the maintenance of global air routes will be made much easier by their existence. In the event of war, their value to combat air forces is hard to overestimate. As staging bases, as alternate landing fields for the sake of dispersal, or as emergency landing areas, they offer a wide range of possibilities.

2. *Project Ice Cube*—the investigation of sea ice for use as aircraft landing strips in the establishment of Distant Early Warning (DEW) stations in Arctic Canada.

This project was begun in March, 1955. The only means of transporting initial construction materials and equipment to proposed DEW line sites within the time desired was air transport. Since landing strips were not available at the sites, it was necessary to use ice surfaces for aircraft landings. Because construction equipment was too large and heavy for contractor commercial air transportation, the U.S. Air Force proposed using its largest transport aircraft, the C-124, provided it could be established that sea-ice thicknesses and strengths were sufficient to support C-124 landings, parking, and takeoffs.

The Center was called upon to provide sources of experience and information. SIPRE and ACFEL were known to have conducted scientific investigations on ice strengths for aircraft landings. Both were requested to provide specific information on the necessary thickness of ice for C-124 operations.

To meet this particular problem an ice survey field team was organized. It was composed of arctic specialists who had developed a working knowledge of sea ice through years of field and laboratory experience and scientists from organizations engaged in snow and ice research. Andrew Assur, Squadron Leader Scott Alexander, and Lieutenant Colonel Donald A. Shaw made up the group that studied conditions and recommended the first successful C-124 landing on ice at Cambridge Bay, Northwest Territories [fig. 1]. This successful test landing was followed by approximately 500 landings along the DEW line. Thirty-one ice landing strips on both fresh and salt water were surveyed; 20 were approved for C-124 landings. The remaining 11 were supplied by C-119 and other lighter aircraft. These ice landings permitted construction of the DEW line to begin approximately 6 months earlier than would have been possible if it had been necessary to rely on sea transport.

Figure 1—The first cargo ship of the DEW line airlift is shown after having landed on the ice runway at Cambridge Bay.

A 17-page report of the project was published by the Center.[15]

3. Reference aid—the Glossary of Arctic and Subarctic Terms.[16]

This glossary was prepared primarily for military personnel and others who are unfamiliar with the specialized vocabularies of arctic literature. The compilation of terms and their definitions is aimed, not at any standardization, but rather at the understanding of the terms and their usage. The compilation of the glossary, which contains about 4,000 terms, represents the combined efforts of 4 contracting institutions, 75 consultants, and 5 staff and 8 clerical members of the Center. The fields covered most adequately include astronomy, anthropology, botany, ecology, geology, geography, glaciology, snow and ice, meteorology, ornithology, mammalogy, sea-ice navigation, and exploration.

[15] Lieutenant Colonel Donald A. Shaw, *Project 572, The Use of Ice for Aircraft Landing Strips* (Maxwell Air Force Base, Ala., 1955). See also ADTIC "History Files," January-June, 1955, Maxwell Air Force Base, Ala.

[16] *Glossary of Arctic and Subarctic Terms*, ADTIC Publication A-105 (Maxwell Air Force Base, Ala., 1955).

4. Life support studies—research for and preparation of studies pertaining to emergency living in the Arctic, physiological and psychological stresses imposed by cold environments and isolation, and the ethnic characteristics of circumpolar peoples. Chief among these are:

a. An analysis of 641 arctic survival experiences.[17] The topical approach used in this study gives an insight into the breadth of experiences and activities of survivors. It is a factual report of what happened to men isolated in the Arctic.
b. A comprehensive survival manual covering emergency living in all areas, including the Arctic.[18]
c. Training films on emergency living in the Arctic.[19]
d. Ethnic studies of the peoples of Siberia, Kamchatka, and the northern parts of the Soviet Union.[20]
e. A detailed analysis of the nature, distribution, and availability of water and food sources in the Arctic; of the techniques and equipment that man has used in obtaining these commodities from snow, ice, and permafrost; and of the changes in requirements, sources, and techniques that have taken place in the quest for food and water.[21]

As of this date (1967), the Center has served the Armed Forces for twenty-five years as a depository of information on nontemperate environments. It is prepared to handle requests for any and all types of information bearing on the fundamental character of environment as related to material, personnel, operational techniques, and requirements. In addition to its information-collecting activities, the Center is conducting research on several long-range projects. Chief among these is the Spacecraft Emergency Land-landing Area Study (SELAS), a study concerned with the selection of land areas that could be used for emergency landing and recovery of manned spacecraft.

[17] Richard A. Howard, *Down in the North,* ADTIC Publication A-103 (Gunter Air Force Base, Ala., 1953).
[18] *Survival,* Air Force Manual 64-5 (St. Louis, 1952 and later editions).
[19] *Survival on Polar Sea Ice,* TF1-4984 (1954); *Survival on the Ice Cap,* TF1-4497 (1955); and *Survival Stresses,* TF1-5375 (1961).
[20] *Ethnic Groups,* ADTIC Publication G-101 (Maxwell Air Force Base, Ala., 1955).
[21] *Man in the Arctic,* ADTIC Publication A-107 (Maxwell Air Force Base, Ala., 1962).

RESPONSIBILITIES OF THE POLAR SCIENTIST-EXPLORER

F. Alton Wade

When a man signs on as a member of a polar expedition, he automatically assumes great responsibilities. This is particularly true of the scientist-explorer. The basic reason for any justifiable expedition is the acquisition and dissemination of knowledge.

Exploration of the polar regions is very costly, more so on the average than for any other region on earth. Of course it is not in the same class with the exploration of outer space. Each bit of information recorded in a data book comes at a very high price. If it remains in the data book and is never made available to fellow scientists and the public, the money has been wasted.

Exploration and scientific research in the polar regions have been in the past and are today financed with funds from two principal sources: Government grants or appropriations and private and institutional donations. When Federal funds are provided for the purpose of exploration, every taxpaying citizen of the country automatically becomes the equivalent of a stockholder in the expedition and has a vested interest in it. Each taxpayer has a right to know what was accomplished by each individual he helped to finance and what new knowledge was forthcoming from each endeavor during the expedition. The scientist-explorer's responsibilities are perhaps to fewer individuals when the funds are provided by individuals, corporations, and institutions, but they are there. A man who "sits on his data," who never publishes the results of his endeavors, is as much a criminal as one who robs a bank.

The taxpayer, the individual, or the corporation has purchased the knowledge gained on an expedition and has a right to this knowledge. Unless the results, the analyses of data, the conclusions, and the theories and speculations are made available by means of publication in journals of high stature, the scientist-explorer is not fulfilling his obligations.

Circumstances vary from expedition to expedition, and there are two sides to every story. There are times when it is very difficult, perhaps impossible, for a man to fulfill his obligations, but no stone should remain unturned by him or his colleagues in the effort to discharge his responsibilities to mankind.

An examination of the accounts, records, and publications of past expeditions shows that the scientist-explorers of some expeditions have nearly perfect records, while those of others have fulfilled their obligations to varying degrees. The latter should not be condemned until the extenuating circumstances are known in each case.

In many instances the finger of guilt should be pointed at the leaders and sponsors of the expedition rather than at the scientist-explorers. Too many times in the past no provisions were made for the post-expedition work, which ultimately results in the desired publications. Funds were raised or granted for carrying out the exploration and scientific projects in the polar regions, but when that phase was over, many scientists had to assume full financial responsibility for completing their tasks in the laboratory and the office. Funds for this phase of the work were negligible or nonexisting in many cases.

For an example of what can happen, let us examine the records of one expedition, the United States Antarctic Service (USAS) Expedition, 1939-41. It was authorized by the Congress of the United States, and Federal funds were appropriated for its needs. These were inadequate for the mission, and only because of supplementary donations by individuals and corporations was it possible to carry out the planned program of exploration and research in the field. At the start no funds were in sight for the post-exploration duties and the preparation of reports for publication.

This was corrected to a very minor degree by extending the life of the USAS for approximately six months after the expedition's return to the United States and by continuing the employment of a few people in order to transcribe completely some journals and prepare maps and nonscientific reports. A few scientists were retained for periods ranging from two weeks to six months. However, with a few exceptions, it was up to the scientists to complete their work and pre-pare their reports on their own. For example: three geologists were included on the staff of the West Base unit (Little America III). Fortunately, two of them were studying for advanced degrees. One made his investigations in Byrd Land the subject of his doctoral dissertation, and a very complete, comprehensive report was the result. The second used his investigations as the subject of his master's thesis. The third geologist was a full-time university professor; his laboratory investigations and subsequent reports were made and prepared during time stolen from the university and during afterhours. The meteorologist was more fortunate. He continued in the employ of the Weather Bureau and was given time and assistance to complete the analysis of his data and prepare his reports for publication. The geophysicist lost his life in an airplane crash during the early days of our participation in World War II, but had he lived he would have had to complete his obligations through his own efforts. Some final reports in some disciplines have not been written to this day.

In fairness it must be pointed out that this expedition returned at a time when all thoughts were concentrated on World War II, which was raging on the east side of the Atlantic and into which we were soon to be drawn. Projects such as the USAS were shelved. It is quite possible that under more normal circumstances Congress would have provided the funds necessary to complete and publish the reports. This, however, is problematical. Support for the glamorous phase of an expedition has always been more easy to obtain than for the non-glamorous, seldom-publicized afterwork that leads to publications.

Some scientist-explorers are more fortunate than others. As an example let us use a geologist from the staff of the U.S. Geological Survey. A grant is obtained to support the project which he proposes to carry on in Antarctica, and provisions are made for time and facilities to prepare his reports once he has returned from Antarctica. In order to get the results of his endeavors into print, an outlet is provided in the *Professional Papers* of the Survey. As a result, there is a minimum of time between the completion of his fieldwork and the publication of the results of that work. This is a most desirable situation.

Scientists representing polar institutes are somewhat less fortunate. They, too are provided time and facilities to complete their reports, but such institutes are for the most part dependent upon grants for their existence and, if these are not forthcoming, projects may be terminated prematurely. These institutes provide outlets for reports in their research series, which are published at irregular intervals. By this method more complete, more detailed reports containing more raw data are made available. The distribution of such reports, however, is of necessity quite restricted.

The least fortunate scientist-explorer is the university professor. The responsibility for a project is his from start to finish. He formulates the project; gets financial support in the form of a grant; obtains a leave-of-absence from his regular duties during the polar field season; and returns with his data, which he proceeds to work up on a part-time basis with many interruptions. Grant support usually runs out before the project is completed, and supplementary support may or may not be forthcoming. When the report is completed, the scientist must then find an outlet in a reputable journal. This is a time-consuming and often disheartening project in itself. Editors of journals are deluged with articles in increasing numbers each year. There is not room for all, and the process of picking and choosing may eliminate his article. If this happens, the process is repeated with a second journal, and so on. When finally accepted, the article then reposes in a file waiting its turn. It may appear within a year after receipt by the editor, although a delay of fifteen months or more is not unusual with some periodicals. Because of space limitations, articles are generally watered down, thus reducing their values. Some appear in journals with very limited circulation. Fortunately, the process of reviewing the literature has been made simple by the splendid abstract service of the Library of Congress.

During the last decade there have been many changes in the opportunities for and the methods of polar exploration and research. Many individuals may now participate in these activities who would have been denied the opportunity ten or more years ago. In the old days of exploration by expeditions at very irregular and infrequent intervals, very few scientists could participate. Those who did were an unusual breed of men. Scientists in many disciplines had to be willing to sacrifice eighteen months or more of their lives in order to do the equivalent of one month's work at home or in more accessible regions. They also had to be willing and able to perform tasks each day throughout the expedition that were strictly hard physical labor totally unrelated to the job for which they had signed on. Great hardships were endured. Each bit of new knowledge came at a very high price. Most of the scientists on early expeditions realized this and fulfilled their obligations by writing and publishing complete reports, including much of the raw data. Most of them were young men with little experience or background beyond a college education, but they had the physical endurance necessary for the inevitable hardships of early expeditions. As the records show, most of them became leaders in their particular branches of science later in life. This is a tribute to the men who chose them for these expeditions.

Today the gates are open to a much larger group of scientists. With strategically located year-round bases and transportation by aircraft available at frequent intervals during the summer season, a scientist may now go to the Antarctic and concentrate on his project for just as long as it takes to do the job. He has no or few housekeeping responsibilities. Every effort is made by support groups to relieve him of all duties not directly related to his project. Every effort is made to make his stay in Antarctica as comfortable as possible. Under these conditions not only are the men who would have qualified for the early expeditions available, but also those who would not have volunteered for those expeditions because of the time element and the physical labor and discomforts involved.

Because of the relative ease with which a man is put in his geographical area of research in the polar regions today, he may not fully realize his responsibilities to the taxpayers who are supporting him. How many scientists who spend a part or even a full summer season in Antarctica on a $20,000 grant fully realize that that amount represents about one-tenth of the actual cost to the taxpayer. If he shirks his duty and does not carry his project through to publication, he is cheating his friends and neighbors.

In the old days every man of an expedition was made aware of nearly every phase of the tremendous effort necessary to put him and his associates in the field. Today this is not true. This is unfortunate since the uninformed scientist may not realize his full responsibilities.

In recent years I have noted that some polar scientists are impatient and highly critical of the support given to their pet project. They are the ones who should not be there. It still takes a special breed of man for work in the polar regions. In addition to their specialized knowledge, they must possess other qualifications. A sense of humor is a must. They must be patient and willing to perform all sorts of tasks related or totally unrelated to their scientific investigations, and do so cheerfully.

It is interesting to compare the conditions under which a polar scientist worked three or so decades ago with the conditions today. Because I am most familiar with the work of the reconnaissance geologist in Antarctica and got my baptism in this work in 1934, and because I continued this type of work as recently as 1966, I use this discipline as an example.

The second Byrd expedition sailed from Boston in October, 1933. Three months later, almost to the day, the Ross Ice Shelf was sighted, and shortly thereafter we landed at Little America. During that interval, I, a geologist, served in many capacities—mess cook, caretaker of the sledge dogs, seaman, and sledge builder to name just a few. Assisting in the construction of Little America II, in the transportation of supplies from unloading points to that camp, and in the night watch occupied my time until well into the winter night. As a member of the party destined to explore the Ford Ranges in Byrd Land, preparations for that trip occupied my time during the remainder of the winter night. Of course, in addition there was always my share of housekeeping duties to perform. Over a year after leaving Boston, the trail party, under the leadership of Paul A. Siple, left for the unknown lands to the east. After 20 days travel with the dog teams, during which time we averaged slightly over 10 miles per day, we arrived at the first rock outcropping on Mount McKinley, our first goal. I was so glad to see a rock again that I knelt down and planted a kiss on this exposure of beautiful gray granodiorite. During the next 6 weeks we visited and worked northward along a traverse through the ranges. Seventy-seven days after leaving Little America II we returned, and in June, 1935, we were back in the United States. In the 18 months of elapsed time, I had been privileged to geologize during 6 weeks. I acquitted my responsibilities by reporting all my findings in my doctoral dissertation, parts of which were published in scientific journals.

In 1966 I left this country, also in October; 5 days later I was treading the ice of McMurdo Sound in Antarctica at the beginning of a field season, not near the close of one. I was transported in style to the permanent base in a tracklaying vehicle. The quarters provided were clean and comfortable. In order to partake of an excellent meal

I had only to walk a quarter of a mile to the mess hall. I did have to assist in assembling the gear and supplies to be used by the geologists who were included in the Byrd Coast Survey Party, but in this task every assistance was provided. A flight to choose a campsite in the Ford Ranges was made, and shortly thereafter six of us, constituting the advance unit, were unceremoniously off-loaded at the site. Instead of pushing the dogs for 20 days, we were on location in a matter of several hours. Investigations in all branches of science from that site were to be by helicopter, and in a matter of a few days the buildings were erected and all personnel and equipment on hand and ready to go. Unfortunately, during the first day of operations one helicopter crashed. There were no casualties, but one-third of the transportation was eliminated. This necessitated revisions in the operational procedures and less time in the field for each individual. Excellent visibility is a prerequisite to safe helicopter operations in polar regions. Because of weather conditions, flying days were rare. As a matter of record, the geologists in the party were able to carry on the geological survey of the area on only 4½ days during December, and on one of these days transportation was by motor toboggan to nearby peaks. Dog-sledge parties operating in the same general area in 1934 and in 1940 had either traveled or worked the outcrops on 25 days during December. Considerably more area was covered and more peaks were visited in the 4½ days in 1966 than in the previous years, but more detailed work was accomplished by the men of the dog-sledge parties. In these two instances the old and the new methods produced equivalent results. In many areas of Antarctica, however, there are far more days suitable for flying than not, and the modern methods result in great accomplishments with less physical effort. Older, more experienced men should take advantage of the opportunities now open to them in the polar regions.

One final point should be made concerning the responsibilities and the obligations of the scientist-explorer financed by the Government. All data, descriptions, manuscripts, etc. (or authentic copies), plus representative specimens, should eventually be placed in designated depositories where they will be available for perusal and study by any and all interested parties. The reasons for such a procedure are quite obvious. Some documents should be placed in the Center for Polar Archives in this building; others, plus all specimens, should be housed in the Smithsonian Institution. Under present agreements between grantees and the National Science Foundation, this procedure is specified. Participants in Government or privately sponsored expeditions in the past years, however, have not been required to do so. Every effort should be made to induce the scientist-explorer to cooperate in every way possible to make more complete collections. How nice it would be if the researcher could go to one city and have at hand all the backlog of information necessary for his work.

COMMENTS ON POLAR ARCHIVES
AND THEIR USES

Marie Tremaine

Director and Editor of the *Arctic Bibliography* since 1947, Miss Tremaine's work has resulted in one of the finest examples of bibliographic work and an unmatched contribution to the literature of the Arctic. She is also the author of publications on the history of printing, Canadian imprints, and bibliographic science.

Closely connected with the development of polar archives and activities in research and information centers is the control of the published literature on exploration and scientific work in polar regions. It was to provide this control for the northern regions that the Arctic Bibliography *was started twenty years ago. It aims to summarize the narratives and reports of explorers and scientists of the past, including the recent past, and to index their information systematically. Its organization is simple and consistent in fundamentals from volume to volume. From the beginning it has been intended as a desk tool to aquaint the arctic research man with work in fields not his own, as well as the more remote publications in his own field, and to provide access to information on the innumerable localities explored and studied throughout the circumpolar area. Hence it directs attention particularly to material of foreign origin. The continuity of effort in compilation, analysis, and indexing, and the cumulation of references (now approaching 100,000) increases progressively the usefulness of this tool. Its sponsors are to be commended for their foresight and persisting encouragement and support of this rather unglamorous arctic project. I look forward to utilizing the results of similar enlightened sponsorship in the Center for Polar Archives. As its collection is expanded and its fonds are made accessible through calendars, etc., unexpected resources of unforeseen application are sure to come to light. The value of the collection will increase even more than its extent will.*

A certainly unforeseen application of one of the results of Sir Edward Belcher's 1852-54 expedition was made over 100 years later. Belcher abandoned H. M. S. Resolute *in Melville Sound, and the vessel drifted east and south into Davis Strait before being recovered by an arctic whaler. The course of this 16-month drift was considered along with other historic drifts by Moira Dunbar[1] in identifying the course of the Soviet drifting station NORTH POLE 7 after it was abandoned north of Greenland in 1959. Probably one of the most frequently used results of an earlier expedition is Alexander T. von Middendorff's air and ground temperature measurements of 1844-46 in the permafrost area of Siberia, particularly in the 382-foot shaft at Yakutsk.[2] This type of report has obvious applications for baseline data in studies of long-term trends in environmental conditions. Such data are usually given in the original manuscript with a wealth of detail that never sees the light of day in a published report. The survival of such manuscripts ultimately depends on archives. The amplifications of manuscript sources over published reports were noted by J. E. Caswell.[3]*

In the social sciences the early expeditionary narratives have even greater uses to the modern scientist. They may depict aboriginals with precontact customs or a culture then little modified though now greatly changed by modern man's influence. One of the most remarkable of these narratives is about Alaska as seen in the 1840's by Zagoskin, who gives us the earliest detailed account of the natural conditions and inhabitants of the Yukon and Kuskokwim Basins. It is just this year available in a good English translation.[4] I may note in passing that this translation was made not from the original Rus-

---

[1] "The Drift of NORTH POLE 7 After Its Abandonment," Canadian Geographer, VI (winter, 1962), 129-142.

[2] "Geothermische Beobachtungen," Reise in den äussersten Norden u. Osten Sibiriens, 1843-44, I, No. 1 (1847), 83-183.

[3] The Utilization of the Scientific Reports of United States Arctic Expeditions, 1850-1909, Stanford University Technical Report No. 2 (1951).

[4] H. N. Michael, ed., Lieutenant Zagoskin's Travels in Russian America, 1842-1844 (Toronto, 1967).

sian edition but from the modern one, for which Zagoskin's manu-script field notes were used to clarify details and identify data to present-day standards.

Russian archival activity is now rather lively in the north. Regional studies centers, some recently set up, some older, seem to stimulate interest in local history and local service, especially in Siberia and the Far Northeast. They produce papers of good amateur and sometimes professional quality. They make collections of various artifacts. Documents unearthed in old repositories are featured, some for their sidelights on the Great Revolution, of course, but others for data on the Russians' penetration into Siberia; their early administration, trade, and relations with the natives; and settlement. Records of the seventeenth- and eighteenth-century expeditions have been found; for example, some of S. I. Dezhnev, who discovered Bering Strait in 1648, and some logistic records of the Bering expedition that show how local labor and transportation were pressed into service.

I know that our National Archives has a wealth of similar records of U.S. polar explorations. The Center for Polar Archives can now focus attention on them. Private enterprise and personal initiative have long been factors in U.S. arctic activities. One can assume that there are journals, diaries, and logbooks still in private hands and family attics that can be attracted to this new center. Also, many teaching and research institutions, particularly in New England, have little-known records of arctic sojourners and polar navigators. We can hope for a clearinghouse of information on these, too, in the Center for Polar Archives.

SESSION V
Visual Records
of Polar Explorations

CHAIRMAN:

Morton J. Rubin

Currently Deputy Chief, Plans and Requirements Division, Environmental Science Services Administration, Mr. Rubin has worked in meteorology all over the world since graduating from Pennsylvania State College in 1942. He is the author of numerous scientific papers on Southern Hemisphere and antarctic meteorology.

Man records his activities in many forms: journals, diaries, observation tables, logs, maps, artistic sketches, etc. Surely photography is one of the best means by which to record the activities of an expedition and to document research.

The photographic image was recognized by polar explorers as having great potential, but the cost, weight, and handling of the equipment, the built-in problems of the polar environment, and the difficulties of transportation limited the use of photography at first. By the 1880's, however, most of the handicaps had been overcome. The photograph had become an indispensable record of accomplishment by the time the Lady Franklin Bay Expedition, under Lieutenant Adolphus W. Greely, was in the Arctic in 1881.

We do not know who was the first U.S. explorer to use motion picture photography in the polar regions. We do know that early in the twentieth century it became the means by which an explorer could capture the attention of an audience and, thereby, swell the coffers in order to help pay the costs of an expedition. With the advent of the airplane, we were able to advance into aerial photography. The returns from the use of photography in polar regions have been tremendous.

We are fortunate in having Captain Finn Ronne, an explorer who has mastered the art and science of the photographic record, as our speaker for the fifth session.

RONNE ANTARCTIC RESEARCH EXPEDITION, 1946-48

Finn Ronne*

A Norwegian by birth, Captain Ronne became interested in the polar regions at an early age. He was a member of Byrd's second expedition to Antarctica, 1933-35, and second in command of East Base during the U.S. Antarctic Service Expedition, 1939-41. He served in the U.S. Navy during World War II and retired with the rank of Captain in 1961. He organized and led the Ronne Antarctic Research Expedition, 1946-48. During IGY, 1957-58, Captain Ronne was Commanding Officer and Scientific Station Leader of Ellsworth Station in Antarctica.

After returning from the United States Antarctic Service (USAS) Expedition in May, 1941, I received a commission in the United States Navy. Off and on in my spare time I began formulating plans for an expedition to delineate the unexplored Weddell Sea coastline and the unknown area south of the coast and perhaps to find the termination of the mountain axis of the Antarctic Peninsula. Following World War II more of my time and energy were spent with these plans. Eventually, through Congressional action, I obtained from the Navy, on a loan basis, a sturdily constructed, ocean-going wooden tug that we christened the *Port of Beaumont*. From

* At the fifth session of the Conference on U.S. Polar Exploration, Captain Finn Ronne presented an extemporaneous commentary to accompany the showing of many hundreds of feet of motion picture film that he had compiled from his records of three antarctic expeditions. Added to these were arctic scenes from several other sources. Since the film cannot be shown in this volume, he has kindly written the following brief summary of his own expedition, 1946-48, for inclusion.

the Army Air Forces, Office of Research and Development, many articles of equipment were obtained for testing, including three airplanes, camping gear, and numerous types of clothing. By selling the exclusive news rights of the expedition to the North American Newspaper Alliance, Inc., and with a few subscriptions from interested friends and a contract with the Office of Naval Research for the scientific results to be obtained, I was finally able to get the expedition underway.

Shortly before sailing, at the request of the Department of State, the Postmaster General of the United States swore me in as "Fourth Class Postmaster of the Territory of Antarctica" on December 20, 1946. Thus I became the first U.S. postmaster to take up duties on that continent.

On March 12, 1947, we anchored in Marguerite Bay off Stonington Island in order to reoccupy the base of the 1939-41 USAS Expedition [fig. 1]. Shortly before leaving the United States the previous January, I had learned through the Department of State that the British Government had established a permanent base on the island two years before. When we arrived at Stonington Island we were met by the British leader, Major K. S. Pierce Butler. The British camp had been constructed about 200 yards from the U.S. camp; later cooperation between the two parties made the distance seem even less.

Later in March we steamed south to establish an operational base at the southeast corner of George VI Sound, 300 miles away. Huge flat-topped icebergs that had broken off the coastal shelf blocked our southern passage. We were therefore unable to make a landing and to deposit the cache of food and gasoline. When we returned to Marguerite Bay we moored the *Port of Beaumont* in a cove one-third of a mile from the base. As temperatures fell during the first week of May, it became safely frozen in the bay ice. It remained there until the summer thaw the following year.

The winter passed rapidly. On July 15 I took a sledge party up to the Antarctic Peninsula plateau, 6,000 feet high, 17 miles east of our base, to establish a meteorological station. This station was manned and operated during the entire flying season and, in conjunction with a station later established near Cape Keeler (125 miles south on the Weddell Sea side of the peninsula), made it possible

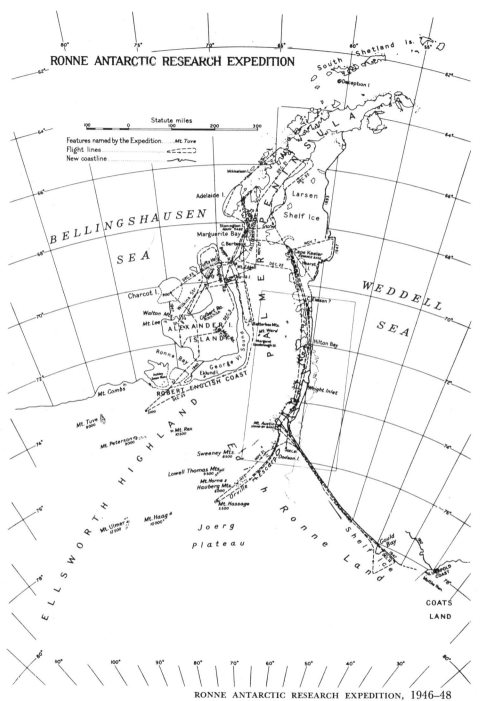

RONNE ANTARCTIC RESEARCH EXPEDITION, 1946–48

Figure 1—The area explored during the Ronne Antarctic Research Expedition, 1946-48.

for H. C. Peterson, our meteorologist, to forecast the highly variable weather with good accuracy.

By August all three airplanes had been unloaded from the ship, assembled, and made ready. On September 29 a short break in the overcast weather allowed Lieutenant Charles J. Adams to fly Walter Smith and C. O. Fiske across the peninsula to establish our second weather station and advance base near Cape Keeler.

During the winter Major Butler and I decided to cooperate in a surface field program. A joint British-American Weddell coast sledge party consisting of four men (Butler and Douglas Mason from the British camp, Walter Smith and Arthur Owen from the U.S. camp) were to cross the peninsula plateau by dog team and then sledge south along the Weddell coast as far south as Mount Tricorn. From this point the two Americans were to continue southward as far as supplies would permit in order to establish ground-control points for our aerial mapping. Our Norseman plane was to drop several caches of supplies along the planned route of the surface party. On October 9, 1947, three of the men of this party left the main base on Stonington Island; Smith joined them at the Cape Keeler station. The party returned to the main base on January 22, 1948, having covered 1,180 statute miles in 105 days on the trail, and having obtained valuable surface fixes to mountains and other features that we photographed from the air on all of our flights in the Weddell Sea coastal area.

On September 28, 1947, the geological party, consisting of Robert L. Nichols and Robert H. T. Dodson, left the main base for George VI Sound. Numerous airplane flights provided this party with food and supplies so they were able to spend 90 days in the field. This allowed them to make a detailed study of the geology in the area they covered. They returned to the main base on December 26 after having covered 450 miles.

By November 7, 1947, the complement of the Cape Keeler station had increased to eight men: the two permanent residents, Fiske and E. A. Wood, and the six in the aviation group, Captain James W. Lassiter, Adams, William R. Latady, Commander Isaac Schlossbach, James B. Robertson, and myself. The tents of the station had originally been pitched on the surface, but heavy drifts soon snowed them over. Series of interconnecting tunnels were dug to facilitate our life underground. Twenty-eight drums of high-octane gasoline were deposited at the station in November for resupply of the airplanes before taking off southward into the unknown.

Heavily overcast weather prohibited a long flight to the south until November 21, 1947. Weather reports radioed from the main base, the plateau weather station, and the sledge party (now 200 miles to the south of us) indicated that this was a perfect day for a long southern flight. The cargo-carrying Norseman, with Adams as pilot and Schlossbach as copilot, headed south with five drums of gasoline. Our twin-engine Beechcraft, equipped with trimetrogon cameras, took off with Lassiter as pilot, Latady as aerial photographer, and myself as navigator.

The visibility was perfect. To the west of our flight track I saw several high, well-defined mountains that were named Owen Peak, the Gutenko Mountains, and Mount Coman. Continuous radio contact was maintained between the two planes as well as with the Cape Keeler station and the main base. About 80 miles south of Mount Tricorn we came upon a large bay, some 55 miles long and 25 miles wide, that was named Gardner Inlet. Almost in the center of the bay, on a low-lying peninsula, was a snow-covered dome mountain 3,200 feet high. It was named Mount Austin. Both planes landed next to Mount Austin since Adams had used half of his gasoline supply and since the mountain was easily recognizable from the air and would therefore serve excellently as a flight standby base [fig. 2]. We were now 250 miles farther south on the Weddell coast

FIGURE 2—The first landing at Mount Austin, November 21, 1947.

than anyone had ever been before. When 2½ drums of gasoline had been transferred from the Norseman's cargo into the tanks of the Beechcraft, we took off. Adams and Schlossbach were left with the Norseman and a trail radio to serve as a safety and emergency cover for our flight.

We climbed to 10,000 feet so that the trimetrogon cameras could photograph the terrain from one horizon to the other. Visibility was unlimited as we followed the trend of the mountainous coastline, which unexpectedly turned westward. To the right of our flight path, numerous mountains of various heights came into view. Mount Haag was the last mountain peak that we discovered and named.

Our flight so far had proved that the mountain axis of the Antarctic Peninsula gradually swings southwestward to 76°30′ S., 72° W., where it either dies out or merges into a higher plateau that stretches southward (toward Ellsworth Land) as the Joerg Plateau. The elevation of this plateau was found to be approximately 4,000 feet, and it stretched to the limit of our visibility. This was the first of two major discoveries that together seemed to eliminate the possibility of any connection above sea level between the Ross and the Weddell Seas.

Our return flight toward Mount Austin paralleled the outward course 20 miles to the west so that an overlapping set of continuous photographs could be taken. When we were within 30 miles of Mount Austin we turned southeast to follow the ice barrier that trended in that direction. An altitude of 10,000 feet was maintained and trimetrogon photographs were taken throughout the flight. At approximately 77° S., 50° W., Lassiter felt we should return to our standby base since we had reached the outward limit of the plane's fuel supply. We sighted Mount Austin without difficulty and landed alongside Adams and Schlossbach 6¾ hours after having left them.

It was obvious that another flight would be necessary to determine the extension of the shelf ice to the east and its connection with Coats Land. To accomplish this, more gasoline would be needed. Instead of waiting in the field while the Norseman brought several loads of gasoline to us, it seemed more efficient for both planes to return to the Cape Keeler station, refuel, and make a second trip to the south. Therefore, half an hour after we had landed at Mount Austin we were again in the air, headed north. The Beechcraft climbed to 11,000 feet so that Latady could photograph the coastline

with the trimetrogon cameras since he had not done so on the outward trip. Although it was 10 P.M. when we took off, the 24 hours
of polar daylight made it possible for him to get good results.

The second long southern flight began at 5:20 A.M. on December
12, 1947. Several days before, we had flown from Cape Keeler along
the Weddell coast as far south as Wright Inlet before overcast weather
necessitated our landing. We had had to leave Cape Keeler with only
three drums of gasoline rather than the usual five in the Norseman
for later transfer into the tanks of the Beechcraft because the snow
surface had softened and the heavily loaded plane could not take off.
The reduced load of gas made it impossible to undertake as long a
flight as had been planned. Instead of flying due south for some
distance, it was decided to follow the ice shelf southeast to Moltke
Nunataks and Coats Land and then as far south as our gas supply
would allow.

At about 78°25′ S., 44° W., we crossed a deeply indented bay,
about 20 miles by 20 miles, that was named Gould Bay. At the head
of the bay was an icefall, heavily crevassed about a mile or more inland. Tongues of ice protruded into the head of the bay, and the bay
itself was partly filled with small bergs cemented together with sea
ice. The bay would seem to offer a suitable place for landing a
wintering party.

Shortly after crossing the bay overcast skies appeared straight
ahead. About 35 miles west of Moltke Nunataks and 3 hours and 7
minutes after taking off, we had to change our course southwesterly
in order to stay at the edge of the overcast. Since this was the most
important leg of our flight, I scanned the horizon southward into the
unknown with fieldglasses for a break in the surface. None was
visible. About 12 miles south of the edge of the ice shelf, Latady obtained a reading from the radio altimeter that indicated the surface
beneath us was 700 feet above sea level. As we flew northwesterly
another reading of the altimeter indicated the surface was now 300
feet above sea level. A final reading at the edge of the ice shelf
showed only 100 feet. The gradual southward increase in elevation
of this huge ice mass was our second important discovery. It, along
with the observations made during the November 21 flight, indicated
the Antarctic Continent is not divided by a frozen body of water
extending from the Ross Sea to the Weddell Sea.

Three and a half hours after taking off we began our return

trip. We had followed for 450 miles the ice barrier that bounds the Weddell Sea on the south and had found that it connects with Coats Land at some distance south of 77°50′ S., 36° W. As we flew north from Mount Austin, Latady took a second set of trimetrogon photographs of the coastline. We landed at the main base on Stonington Island the evening of December 12, having been in the air over 12 hours and having covered 1,700 miles.

In addition to the two long southern flights along the Weddell Sea, trimetrogon flights were made over the west and east sides of the Antarctic Peninsula both north and south of the main base. The first of these flights took off on December 23, 1947, with ceiling and visibility unlimited. We flew south past Mount Edgell at the entrance of George VI Sound and followed the westward trend of English Coast to Ronne Entrance where the sound terminates.

While viewing the antarctic scenery from the air, my thoughts drifted back to my long sledge journey over this area 7 years earlier. The Main Southern Sledge Party [fig. 3], consisting of 7 men and

FIGURE 3—The Main Southern Sledge Party, consisting of (left to right) Finn Ronne, Carl Eklund, Lytton Musselman, Paul Knowles, Joseph Healy, Donald Hilton, and Glenn Dyer.

PHOTO BY ARTHUR J. CARROLL, U.S. ANTARCTIC SERVICE

55 huskies, had left the USAS Expedition East Base on November 6, 1940. By November 21 we had reached an elevation of 7,300 feet on the peninsular plateau (about 150 miles south of East Base), and the supporting party had been released to return to base. My companion, Carl R. Eklund, and I had started off fresh with 15 dogs and enough supplies for 74 additional days in the field.

During the sledge journey 460 miles of new coastline had been discovered and surveyed. Our major discovery had been the western extension of George VI Sound, which terminates in an open sea. This discovery had proved "Alexander I Land" actually to be an island and thus had eliminated Admiral Bellingshausen's (of the Russian Navy) claim to have seen part of the Antarctic Continent. What he actually had seen when sailing past the rocky coast in 1821 was an island separated from the mainland by an ice-filled strait.

During our 84 days in the field, Eklund and I had traveled a total of 1,264 statute miles in 61 actual days of sledging—an average of 20.7 miles per day. The longest journey in any one day had been 42.5 statute miles.

Our main objective on the sledge trip had been geographical exploration and the establishment of the ground-control points that are essential for aerial mapping operations. It is a well-known fact that an aerial photograph may be beautiful to look at, but it is worthless for mapping purposes unless it is tied in with accurately established control points on the surface. These ground-control points may be mountains, sharp rock outcrops, striking icefalls, or anything else whose accurate location has been determined in terms of latitude and longitude and whose size or color guarantees that it will be seen from the air and recorded in the trimetrogon photographs of the area. Once the exact location of such a feature has been determined, photographs of the feature are taken from the ground with accurate bearings to it from fixed observation sites.

During our sledge journey a total of 34 astronomically fixed observation sites had been established for 12 principal control features. At these sites complete photographic circles had been taken at 30° changes in azimuth, thereby making certain that the pictures were overlapping. This had assured that some features would appear in two photographs. From these features, then, the positions of 320 major mountain peaks and nunataks had been determined. Elevations

FIGURE 4—An aerial photograph of mountains in Palmer Land taken during the December 23, 1947, flight. The mountains were later identified by tying them to ground-control points obtained and photographed by Ronne and Eklund during their 1940 sledge trip.

had also been determined for all these features based upon the barometer elevations of the observing sites.

With the three electrically operated cameras mounted in the plane on the December 23, 1947, flight, it was possible to cover the entire area of the flight track from horizon to horizon. The three pictures taken simultaneously had an overlap of about 60 percent, thus assuring complete coverage. Pictures were taken every 15 seconds. While flying over this area I could identify most of the major features that had been discovered and photographed from the ground in 1940. Later the ground and aerial photographs were tied together for the purpose of accurate mapping [fig. 4].

At the turning point of the December 23 flight, the radio altimeter recorded a surface elevation of 3,100 feet. The surface appeared smooth, and we decided to land. The line of position I obtained from sun shots upon landing provided other ground control for the photographs we had just taken in the air [fig. 5].

Returning toward base we landed on the highly elusive Charcot Island, about 20 miles south of the three small mountain peaks on

FIGURE 5—Ronne and Lassiter obtaining line of position by sun observation at the landing in the unknown south of English Coast, December 23, 1947.

the island. The sun was due west of us, therefore a good longitudinal line was obtained that indicated the westernmost landing we made.

Other trimetrogon flights were made over the areas north and south of the base during the few days with weather suitable for flying. For the entire expedition, a conservative total of 250,000 square miles of heretofore unexplored terrain and 450,000 square miles of terrain that had been explored were accurately photographed for the first time. All results were recorded in over 14,000 aerial photographs. Three hundred and forty-six hours were flown by the three airplanes. No less than 86 landings were made in the field, about half of which were unsupported, to accomplish this program.

In addition to the photographic work, we obtained data in various branches of science. Robert L. Nichols, head of the geology department at Tufts University, spent 154 days in the field. He was ably assisted by Robert H. T. Dodson. Our physicist, H. C. Peterson, worked in meteorology, cosmic rays, solar and surface radiation, refraction, and dew point measurements. C. O. Fiske helped him at the main base and later at the field station that he (Fiske) operated on the Weddell Sea coast near Cape Keeler. Andrew Thompson made continuous seismic recordings and took magnetic readings in addition to operating the first tidal station ever to be erected on the Antarctic Continent.

Pilots Charles J. Adams and James W. Lassiter were assigned to the expedition from the U.S. Air Force. Aerial photographer, William R. Latady, operated the trimetrogon cameras installed in the Beechcraft. He also took still and motion pictures of most expedition activities. Others who took an active part in the expedition's extensive program were Isaac Schlossbach, second in command, Walter Smith, Arthur Owen, James Robertson, Charles Hassage, Mrs. Ronne, and Sigmund Gutenko. We also manned and operated our sturdy 1,200-ton wooden ship during the journey to and from the Antarctic, a distance of more than 14,000 miles [fig. 6]. Of the 23 expedition members, only 8 had ever been at sea before.

At the main base we had a complete photographic laboratory. Electrically operated developing and fixing tanks for processing the aerial film were there as well as an electrically operated dryer. With temperatures far below zero on the outside and with only a small coal-burning stove heating the science building, it was difficult to keep the developing chemicals and rinsing water at an even tempera-

RONNE ANTARCTIC RESEARCH EXPEDITION, 1946–48

FIGURE 6—The *Port of Beaumont* before returning to the United States, with the expedition's base in the background.

ture. Each roll of film used in aerial photography contained 250 exposures. All 60 rolls of this film were turned over to the U.S. Air Force. Some of the film has been used in producing maps of some of the areas we covered on our flights.

I believe it is very important to obtain a complete photographic record of every aspect of a polar expedition. In this we were exceedingly successful. Supplementing our records of scientific data, which were published by the Office of Naval Research, all flight and ship logs, journals, and still and motion picture coverage will provide ideal reference material for the future researcher. Much photographic material as well as other records of value from many United States expeditions are scattered all over the land. If all materials of this nature were preserved at the Center for Polar Archives, an inestimable contribution to future students of polar matters would be made.

CONCLUDING SESSION
REMARKS

Robert H. Bahmer
Archivist of the United States, 1966–68

I want to thank you on behalf of the General Services Administration and the National Archives for coming to this, the final session of this conference. It has been a long day devoted to the discussion of polar exploration for those of you who arrived early this morning for the first conference session. Your attendance is the highest possible honor for the opening of the Center for Polar Archives.

Tonight you are present at the opening of a second feature of the conference—an exhibit, in the Constitution Avenue foyer, devoted to polar exploration. If you have not already seen it, I hope you will do so at the close of this session.

It is not surprising in this day and age of instant communication and transportation that your colleagues in both polar regions know about this conference and have sent greetings to you. I would like to read their messages. From Ralph A. Lenton, leader of Project Blue Ice *in the Arctic:*

> Best wishes on the occassion [sic] of the formal opening of the Center for Polar Archivas [sic] from the Arctic Institute of North America personnel at Inge Lehmann Station located at seventy eight degrees North latitude thirty nine degrees West longitude on the Greenland ice cap.

From Richard B. Weininger, Station Scientific Leader, and Lieutenant Ronald C. Sullivan, MC, USN, Officer-in-Charge, Amundsen-Scott South Pole Station:

> Scientific and Naval personnel at geographic South Pole delighted at establishment of the Center for Polar Archives to make available records of United States achievements in both polar regions. Believe our activities will in future form a small but significant addition to the record. Regret winter night makes impossible our attendance at opening ceremony but greetings to all present and best wishes for continued success of the Center.

From Captain W. Benkert, USCG cutter Eastwind:

> Presently conducting oceanographic survey operations in the Kara Sea, send warmest greetings to all partcipants [sic] in the polar exploration conference. We would particularly like to convey our best wishes to those of you with whom we have had the pleasure of sailing. Wish we were there.

From Trevor Lloyd, Chairman of the Board of Governors of the Arctic Institute:

> Returning from Greenland today have seen kind invitation attend conference on polar exploration. Regret inability to be present but desire congratulate National Archives important step establishing Center for Polar Archives. Look forward close cooperation between it and Arctic Institute of North America.

From Admiral Willard T. Smith, Commandant of the U.S. Coast Guard in Washington:

> The United States Coast Guard congratulates the National Archives for the great contribution to the study of polar exploration evidenced by the establishment of "The Center for Polar Archives."
>
> Maintaining records of polar exploration and research will prove invaluable in the future, and is an excellent living memorial to those who have sacrificed so much to provide the information already gathered.
>
> The Coast Guard will be most pleased to assist the Center in obtaining pertinent polar information as we continue our work in this important field. We also plan to make use of the information now at hand at the Center to give us further insight and vision to the potentials of the Polar areas.

On behalf of the U.S. Coast Guard, I wish the National Archives, and its many supporters, best wishes on this wonderful and challenging endeavor.[1]

It pleases us greatly, of course, to receive that kind of word.

I would like to turn this session over to the gentleman in the U.S. Government who oversees the operations of the National Archives and Records Service. He is a man who has spent his whole life in public service; I refer to the very sympathetic boss I have, the able Administrator of General Services, Lawson B. Knott, Jr.

[1] These messages are among the records of the Conference on U.S. Polar Exploration, Record Group 64, Records of the National Archives and Records Service, National Archives.

INTRODUCTION OF A. LINCOLN WASHBURN

Lawson B. Knott, Jr.

Administrator of General Services, 1965-69

It has been a pleasure for GSA to host the conference sessions that so many of you participated in earlier today. I recognize many of you here tonight. Even though it has been a long day, I am certain that it has been a worthwhile one. The greetings that were just read must be heart-warming to those of you who have experienced polar adventures in times past.

Our speaker this evening is both an explorer and a scientist. He began his career in exploration as a member of the Harvard-Dartmouth Mount Crillon Expedition in Alaska in 1934 while still an undergraduate at Dartmouth College. He joined the National Geographic Society's Mount McKinley Expedition in 1936, the year after he received his bachelor's degree from Dartmouth. That same year he was a member of the U.S. Olympic Ski Team. From the time he served as assistant geologist on the Louise A. Boyd East Greenland Expedition in 1937, he annually explored in the North American Arctic until service in the Air Corps during World War II interrupted these activities. On his return to civilian life, he became the first executive director of the Arctic Institute of North America, a position he held until 1951. His academic career has taken him from McGill University to Dartmouth to Yale, where he was professor of geology from 1960 to 1966. Regularly consulted by the U.S. Government on his specialties, geomorphology and glacial geology, he is a Fellow of the American Geographical Society and a member of its governing council, a member of the Geological Society of America, of the Arctic Institute of North America, of the American Geophysi-cal Union, and of Sigma Xi.

Ladies and gentlemen, I present our distinguished speaker, Dr. Albert Lincoln Washburn, professor of geology and now director of the Quaternary Research Center of the University of Washington. He will speak to us on the subject, "Polar Research: Some Issues." Dr. Washburn, it is a great pleasure to have you with us.

POLAR RESEARCH: SOME ISSUES

A. Lincoln Washburn

Dr. Washburn has served as professor of geology and Director of the Quaternary Research Center of the University of Washington since 1966. In 1937 he was assistant geologist on the Louise A. Boyd East Greenland Expedition, and he explored annually in the North American Arctic until serving in World War II. Returning to civilian life after the war, he became the first executive director of the Arctic Institute of North America, a position he held until 1951. He has taught at McGill and Dartmouth Universities, and was a professor of geology at Yale from 1960 to 1966. In addition to his present duties with the University of Washington, he is also Senior Research Associate at Yale University.

I want to express my deep appreciation for the invitation to be here with you. I am honored to be speaking to this distinguished group amid these inspiring surroundings, which emphasize the significance of the occasion—the inauguration of an archival center to assure the safeguarding of polar records relating to many of the expeditions we have heard about today. The work of the Center for Polar Archives is close to many of us, for the center contains not only the records of colleagues who have left on their last and greatest expedition, but also the records of many friends who are here tonight, whose work and generosity we are also honoring. The value of the center to our country is obvious, and those who established it are to be congratulated.

The director of the center is a friend and colleague from World War II days when we worked together in the Air Force's Arctic, Desert, and Tropic Information Center. I speak for him, too, when I say we wish our chief at that time, Laurence M. Gould, could be here with us. Larry was originally scheduled to speak this evening, but he had a conflicting engagement he could not break. He has asked me to extend his regrets and very best wishes to this group—one of the most representative gatherings of U.S. polar workers ever brought together.

In discussing polar research in the time available, I shall not deal with individual disciplines or research fields but with more general matters. However, before I finish I hope I can be sufficiently specific, and perhaps provocative, to stimulate consideration of certain issues. Some of these have already been touched upon by today's speakers. In this discussion I shall use the term "polar" in a loose sense; this usage will not affect the issues.

The history of U.S. polar exploration has been well covered in today's presentations, and I shall not dwell on historical aspects of polar research except to cite some facets and changes as they affect the issues I have in mind. I am particularly concerned with the future, and, without forecasting trends, I shall raise some questions and make several personal observations as I go along. I emphasize the adjective *personal,* especially in the case of views you may find ill advised!

Science has many aspects. We have basic and applied science, although the distinction is not always clear, and we have the broad groupings of the biological, physical, and social sciences. All these aspects are involved in polar research, which I shall equate with investigation in some field of science either in the polar regions or very closely related to polar problems.

Many types of motivation and activity have been represented. Much geographical research has been stimulated by the prospect of economic gain, as in the search for the Northwest Passage by many early expeditions or in the penetration of the Canadian Arctic by the Hudson's Bay Company. Some science has been a product of expeditions primarily motivated by personal or national prestige. Unpublicized efforts, such as routine Government surveys in Alaska, have produced some fine research; and certain Government investigations motivated primarily by national defense interests and requirements have also led to broad scientific accomplishments as shown, for instance, by the glaciological work of the Army's Cold Regions Research and Engineering Laboratory and of the Navy Electronics Laboratory, the arctic program of the Office of Naval Research (ONR), and some Air Force investigations. Such activities have not been motivated primarily by science for science's sake, but a number have resulted in good science. Others have been less productive in this regard. Certainly science for science's sake has not necessarily been the guiding motivation for polar research.

The approach in which science for science's sake, involving full-time research, is the leading motivation was stressed by Karl Weyprecht in 1875[1] and led to the expeditions of the 1882-83 and 1932-33 international polar years. These were followed by the scientifically much more refined and better supported International Geophysical Year (IGY) expeditions of 1957-58. Concurrently, research and logistic costs skyrocketed. The funds expended for IGY logistics necessarily far exceeded those for the research itself. Estimates range from sevenfold to many times more, the exact ratio being difficult to establish because the basis for separating these costs is highly variable.

The *sine qua non* of research, whatever its motivation, is quality. In polar research the stakes are particularly high because of the expensive logistics and the cost of putting a scientist in the field. On the other hand, there is a scarcity of established scientists who can arrange to spend enough time in the field once they get there. The danger of wasting funds on mediocrity is obvious, but the danger must be weighed against the desirability of maintaining a continuing effort and giving younger scientists the opportunity to prove their worth—as many of them have done.

A closely related question is the training of graduate students. Here field research can involve special problems for both faculty and students. In many institutions a professor is expected to seek the financing of a student's research as well as supervise it. So, following a common procedure, the professor develops a project in his own name as chief investigator. However, the professor may be handicapped in finding enough time to visit a student's field area in the Arctic or Antarctic and still do his own research. As a result, the student and project may receive inadequate supervision. Yet, if the student's work is interwoven with the professor's research to the extent

[1] In lectures in Vienna and Graz (cf. Wohlgemuth, E. E. von, *Die internationale Polarforschung, 1882-1883, Die österreichische Polarstation Jan Mayen, Beobachtungsergebnisse: Kaiserliche Akademie der Wissenschaften, Vorbericht,* I (Wien, 1886), 1-4.

that these problems do not arise, there may be too much supervision of the student as well as difficulties in maintaining his project as an independent contribution of Ph.D. caliber.

To summarize, then, full-time research and, I suspect, basic research of high caliber are scarcer in the history of polar exploration than one might suppose from frequent expeditionary allusions to scientific programs. Also, the high cost of polar research puts an especially high premium on quality.

Such problems as the difficulty of maintaining high standards in research and in training graduate students reflect the individuality of science in the polar regions. This individuality is characterized by two features: First, the climate; and second, the transportation difficulties imposed by the climate and the distance from civilization.

For some of us, work in polar climates can be far more attractive than work elsewhere, but we are a minority. Even those of us who like polar work are not thereby relieved of expensive and difficult logistics. This high cost of polar research, which F. Alton Wade and others have mentioned today, makes adequate financial support a perennial problem. I am sure that financial considerations are involved when the priorities of VIP's and press representatives visiting the Antarctic sometimes exceed those of working scientists to the detriment of scheduled scientific projects—although perhaps to the advantage of future antarctic programs requiring public support.

In our country a national program of polar research needs a proper balance between public and private backing. Clearly, some programs are almost entirely in the Government domain and are necessarily completely dependent on Government financing, such as large-scale mapping programs and the data-acquisition aspects of polar weather stations. Not only are these programs logical Government responsibilities, but the logistic requirements are so extensive that Government funding is mandatory. Government financing is also essential for most antarctic work, as well as for many arctic programs.

We rely on the Navy for antarctic transportation. We owe much to the Navy for our IGY accomplishments in Antarctica, for in the time then available for planning, little could have been done without Naval manpower, ships, and planes. This support pattern has proved its worth, and it continues to our benefit. As for the future, it would be interesting to see if contractual arrangements with private organizations for part of the research support could be equally productive and efficient on a strict cost-accounting basis. At a polar conference held at Dartmouth College in 1958 I remember Maurice Ewing suggesting that private operation of logistics might be more efficient as well as cheaper for certain research. But even if cheaper, it might entail more difficulty in obtaining the necessary appropriations from Congress since it can be legitimately argued that the Navy as well as science is benefitting from the arrangement. After all, the Navy should maintain a capability for operating in polar seas and has done it splendidly with its transarctic nuclear submarines. Nevertheless, I think if we had an increased capability for private as well as Government operation of antarctic logistics it would provide more flexibility and might be to the advantage of polar research in this country.

In the Arctic, on the other hand, the private sector is much more active logistically. This is illustrated by extensive construction projects and oil exploration ventures as well as by Government contracts with private organizations for servicing facilities—for instance, the arrangement between ONR and the University of Alaska for operating the Naval Arctic Research Laboratory (NARL) at Point Barrow.

In the strictly scientific aspects, too, we see the majority of funds coming from our Government, but here there is a significant mixture of Government and private operation of programs. A geological project in the Antarctic, for example, may be carried out by the U.S. Geological Survey or by a Government-financed university group. This is a healthy situation, but I wish there were more financial aid from private sources. In the old days the private sector was very active in funding polar research, perhaps because the expeditionary aspects were then more glamorous. Today polar research is pretty much of a routine, albeit expensive, business.

As a result, even private research groups must rely on Government grants for much of their work, and it is to the credit of our Government that high-caliber research can generally be funded. Yet private organizations cannot rely on Government funding alone and remain healthy. In order to survive, some organizations find themselves on a treadmill of paperwork where they spend too much of their time preparing research proposals. Often these are unrelated to each other and designed to fit programs of a variety of agencies rather than being focused on more thoughtful and better-integrated projects. Moreover, organizations operated largely by Government funds might be forced to fold completely in the event of a particularly sudden and drastic economy move. In addition, there is danger of organizations being unduly pressured to take on work that is perhaps detrimental to their primary function. This is illustrated by recent criticism of the reluctance of some educational institutions to undertake classified work. Some Congressmen—I hope a very small minority—have even advocated that the Department of Defense make such institutions see the error of their ways by withdrawing all defense work from them, including unclassified and basic research of possible benefit to defense agencies.[2] The greatest protection here is adequate free income or endowment for private research groups. I do not see the outlook for this kind of support improving for polar research, although such support is essential if research is to maintain a reasonable degree of independent strength.

Again, to summarize before proceeding further: it seems to me the high cost of polar research makes such research increasingly difficult to undertake without Government financing. This in turn creates issues for both the Government and the private sector, and some dangers for the latter.

I am also interested in the question of whether future polar research should stress an area-study approach or a discipline approach. Historically, the area emphasis has been dominant, and the term "polar research" suggests that this is still true. But as logistics improve there is less need for polar experts or specialists; therefore, I see more need for private and Government polar groups to continually reexamine their missions and operations in the light of the times. I am not questioning the value of area studies as such—far from it. Rather I wish to stress that polar research is taking on new dimensions. To the extent that there is less need for experts and that work in polar regions is becoming more routine, polar research is becoming more like any other scientific investigation that lends itself to an area emphasis. Very few basic research problems are peculiar to a polar environment in the sense of being distinctly different in substance as opposed to being different in degree or scale. The Antarctic ice sheet, the Greenland ice sheet, and widespread perma-

[2] E. L., "Secret Research: Tightrope Act on Capital Hill," *Science*, CLVI (June, 1967), 1,718.

frost are peculiarly polar, but these features are unique mainly because of their wide areal extent. From the disciplinary viewpoint, the area aspects are in a sense variations on the main theme—science. There is nothing new about such an approach; many of the IGY programs were based on it. Yet this approach merits special attention because it permits a much wider range of interests and talents to be directed toward polar research than just that represented by polar enthusiasts like myself. In fact, it means that polar research will increasingly be done for its wider implications with respect to science as a whole rather than for its area significance alone.

This trend poses a question for the administration of polar research. Should a geological project, for example, be judged and administered by a disciplinary unit, such as the National Science Foundation's (NSF) Earth Sciences Section—or should it be handled on an area basis through the NSF Office of Antarctic Programs or perhaps some future office of polar programs that will also include the Arctic? Should a university group specialize in the polar regions with a staff of its own, or should a polar project be under the aegis of a university department or an interdepartmental research center? These questions are colored various shades of gray. Aside from possible administrative confusion, there is nothing to oppose both types of organization, even at the same institution, as long as high-quality research is maintained. Nevertheless, the administrative complexity remains. One can file a library card under subject and area headings, but a budding research project is not disposed of so easily.

I do not know if administrators will ever resolve the dichotomy between the area type of organization on the one hand and the disciplinary type on the other. Probably both are valid and necessary depending on the circumstances. I suggest, however, that the area type is ideally suited to polar institutes whose traditional function is to bring together scientists who are particularly attracted to polar areas. Such groups should be in an excellent position to organize and carry through comprehensive area studies. On the other hand, the disciplinary type organization may be in the best position to understand and evaluate the implications of a polar research project for science as a whole. In any event, the changing aspects of polar research as they affect its administrative framework constitute another broad issue warranting consideration.

Looking broadly at research itself, I strongly endorse the view

W. J. L. Sladen expressed today about the importance of interdisciplinary and multidisciplinary programs—whether the work stresses area study for its own sake or is approached from the more general disciplinary viewpoint. The distinction in these terms, as I interpret them, is important. To me, multidisciplinary means that more than one discipline is involved in a research project but implies nothing further. Interdisciplinary means that a research project is carried on between disciplines in the sense of cutting across disciplinary boundaries and implies intimate collaboration between researchers. For instance, a botanist and a geologist can study an area quite independently in a multidisciplinary approach but would collaborate very closely in an interdisciplinary study of the effect of frost action and slope movement on plants. An interdisciplinary program thus presents the better integrated approach to a problem. It can be particularly rewarding in polar work where there is special need to make maximum use of the usually limited support facilities.

However, there are inherent dangers that need to be considered in cooperative programs. For example, the very nature of ice-sheet traverses and oceanographic cruises with their tight timetables favors cooperative programs, and it is tempting to crowd as much as possible into them to make the most of the opportunity. The danger, of course, is overscheduling so that projects interfere with each other to the detriment of the overall program. A properly balanced approach is easy to call for but difficult to carry out, and credit is due the NSF in this regard for its successful *Eltanin* operations.

We also need to maintain a proper balance between field and laboratory work. Certain kinds of research can only be carried out in the field; others only in the laboratory; probably the majority of comprehensive efforts require both approaches. To the extent that progress can be planned, which may be impossible in basic research, we should make sure that both approaches are represented at the right time and the right place. I mention these truisms because, for some problems, it may be easier to bring the laboratory and its methods into the field than to simulate field conditions in the laboratory. Moreover, appropriately placed field stations have much to recommend them since some problems need to be investigated by repeated observations at the same place over a period of years. All too often an interpretation of a past event is based on inadequate knowledge of how certain processes operate today, and field stations like

NARL can provide an excellent base for detailed, long-term studies of these processes. Such research is highly valuable and rarer in polar regions than one might think.

Interdisciplinary cooperation can overcome artificial barriers between disciplines and promote a joint focus on problems, but there are still other barriers in the way of scientific progress and full utilization of resources and talent. Were it not for certain unfortunate political facts of life, much closer international collaboration in science could be brought to bear on questions of common interest. We are meeting here today to inaugurate the Center for Polar Archives within the National Archives, and most presentations today have appropriately stressed national aspects of polar work. But science in the broadest sense is not limited by national boundaries. International cooperation can contribute immensely to the best utilization of resources and talent. Scientific cooperation could perhaps also serve an even wider function by leading to other types of cooperation that could be in the long-term self-interest of all nations.

An excellent start has been made in the Antarctic, where IGY set a pattern whose philosophy has been continued by the Scientific Committee on Antarctic Research (SCAR) of the International Council of Scientific Unions. The Arctic is more sensitive politically, but the number of scientific problems offering opportunities for international cooperation are even greater and far less difficult logistically. The Expedition Glaciologique Internationale au Groenland, which has been studying the Greenland ice sheet, is a good example of a joint effort. Canada, the Scandinavian countries, the Union of Soviet Socialist Republics, and the United States have much to gain from cooperation in arctic research, and I think the time has come when we should consider forming an arctic counterpart of SCAR to further this approach. Science in the polar regions will advance regardless of organizational frameworks, but an international arctic research committee modeled on SCAR might stimulate progress.

I have mentioned some changing aspects of polar research and certain issues that concern me: the maintenance of high quality in research and in training graduate students, a proper balance between public and private support of polar research, the high cost and resulting problems for the private sector, the administration of science as it bears on the philosophy of an area study for its own sake as opposed to the significance of areal variations for a discipline, the importance of interdisciplinary programs and of a proper balance between field and laboratory work, and the desirability of international cooperation in arctic as well as antarctic research.

In conclusion I return to the beginning when I said I wanted to stimulate consideration of certain issues, although I did not say why. One reason is that the National Academy of Sciences is making a study in depth of polar research—its status, critical scientific problems, organization, funding, and future trends. Hopefully some of the issues I have raised are sufficiently provocative to generate discussion and ideas that will feed back and benefit this study—and in turn advance polar research. The Center for Polar Archives and all of us here have an important stake in the quality and the future of that research.

INDEX

Abbot, James L.: 41

Adams, Charles J.: 162, 163, 164, 170

Adams, John Quincy: 108

Adélie Penguin (*Pygoscelis adeliae*): 72, 74

Advance: 4

Advisory Committee on Antarctic Names, U.S. Board on Geographic Names: 92, 94, 116. *See also* Antarctic Place Names Committee of the Permanent Committee on Geographic Names of the United Kingdom

Aerial photography: 48, 142, 158, 160, 162, 164, 166, 167, 170. *See also* Photomapping; Wilkins, Sir Hubert; Cartography; Maps; Antarctic Maps and Aerial Photography Library

Aircraft: 14, 15, 16, 48, 51, 57-61, 70-73, 90, 160, 162-164; Balloons, 86, 91, 96; Beechcraft, 83, 163, 164, 165, 170; Cessna–180, 27; C–130 Hercules, 61; C–124, 143; C–119, 143; C–121J Super Constellation, 65; Condor, 83, 87, 94, 95, 98; Helicopter, 51, 53, 66, 71, 152; UH–1B turbine helicopter, 61, 65; LC–130F Hercules, 65; *N–1* (airship), 16; Norseman, 162, 163, 164, 165; P–2V Neptune (LP–2J), 58, 65; R–4D Skytrain, 27, 28, 58; R–5D Skymaster, 58. *See also* Aerial photography; East Base flight programs; Ellsworth, Lincoln; Glacial ice landing fields; Mile High Camp, emergency air evacuation of; Spacecraft Emergency Land-landing Area (SELAS) ; Station Modular Units; West Base flight programs; Wilkins, Sir Hubert

Alabama Packet: 105

Alaska: 26; Area study of, 140; Basic exploration of, 14-15; Exploration for oil in, 19-21; Fairbanks, 22; George M. Stoney and, 15; Patrick H. Ray and, 11; Purchase of, 10; *N–1* (airship) and, 16; Wilkins and Eielson in, 16; Zagoskin's narrative of, 155. *See also* Arctic; Greenland; U.S. Air Force; U.S. Navy; University of Alaska

Alexander, Scott: 143

Alexander I Land: 91, 92, 93, 95, 167

Alexander Island: 92-93, 96, 167

Allen, Henry T.: 15

American Geographical Society: 11, 16, 178; Bulletin of, 13; Cooperation with ADTIC, 142; Library of, 104, 116, 130. *See also* Wilkins, Sir Hubert

American Geophysical Union: 179

American Philosophical Society: 4, 11, 110, 114

Amundsen, Roald: 16, 60

Amundsen-Scott South Pole Station: 60, 176

Anderson, William R.: 25, 31, 32-34

Andree, Salomon A.: 15

Andrew Jackson Mount. *See* Jackson, Mount

Annawan: 103, 105

Antarctic Commission. *See* Richard E. Byrd Antarctic Commission; Byrd, Richard E.

Antarctic Convergence: 101

Antarctic ice sheet: 185

Antarctic Peninsula: 45, 50, 63, 70, 71, 86, 87, 89, 90, 92, 93, 95, 96, 101, 105, 114, 159, 160, 162, 164, 166

Antarctic Peninsula plateau: 160

Antarctica: Aerial conquest of, 57-61, 70-73, 90, 160, 162-164; Biological research in, 70, 71, 73, 76; Biotelemetrical research in, 74; British Antarctic Survey, 1839–43, 71, 111; Establishing the existence of, 45, 111; First documented landing on, 105; First U.S. Postmaster in, 160; Physiological research in, 85. *See also* Advisory Committee on Antarctic Names, U.S. Board on Geographic Names; Antarctica, geographical locations in; U.S. Antarctic Mapping Center; U.S. Antarctic Service (USAS) ; U.S. Antarctic Service Expedition, 1939–41

Antarctica, geographical locations in: Andersen Harbor, 97; Austin, Mount, 163, 164, 166; Batterbee Cache, 93, 94, 95; Batterbee Mountains, 92, 93; Bay of Whales, 85; Beardmore Glacier, 83; Bellingshausen Sea, 92, 94; Bouvet Is-

189

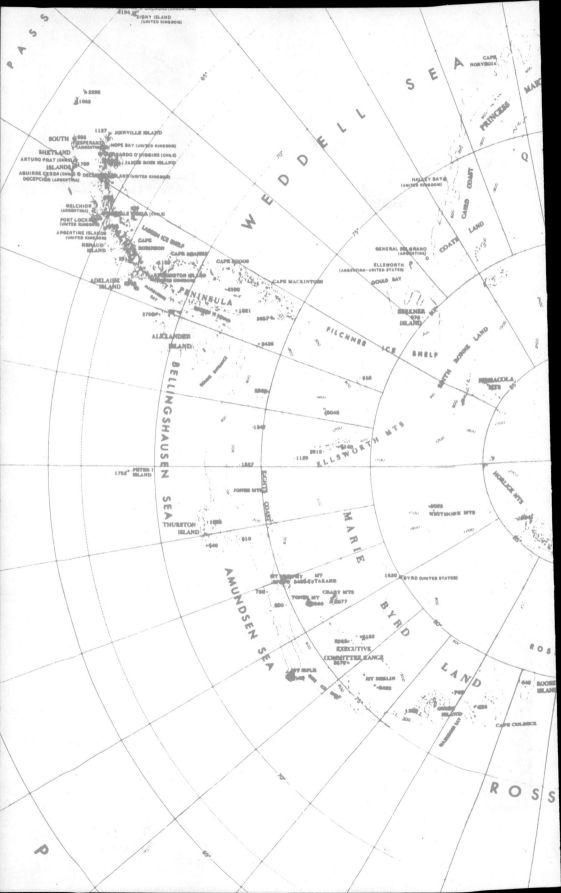